Soups, Salads & Sandwiches

With the Micheff Sisters

A Vegan Vegetarian Cookbook

Also by the Micheff sisters
Cooking With the Micheff Sisters
Cooking Entrees With the Micheff Sisters
Cooking for Two With the Micheff Sisters

Cover recipes: Old Fashioned Vegetable Soup, p. 14;
Crisp Autumn Salad, p. 91; Curried Chicken Salad Sandwich, p. 98

3ABN BOOKS is dedicated to bringing you the best in published materials consistent with the mission of Three Angels Broadcasting Network. Our goal is to uplift Jesus Christ through books, audio, and video materials by our family of 3ABN presenters. Our in-depth Bible study guides, devotionals, biographies, and lifestyle materials promote whole person health and the mending of broken people. For more information, call 618-627-4651 or visit 3ABN's Web site: www.3ABN.org.

Designed by Michelle C. Petz
Portrait photos by Chrystique Neibauer
Recipe photos by Mark Mosrie

Unless otherwise noted all Bible verses are from The New King James Bible Version, copyright © 1979, 1980, 1982, Thomas Nelson Inc., Publishers.

Additional copies of this book are available from two locations:
3ABN: Call 1-800-752-3226 or visit online at www.3ABN.org.
Adventist Book Centers: Call toll-free 1-800-765-6955 or visit online at AdventistBookCenter.com.

ISBN 13: 978-0-8163-2383-8 (pbk.)
ISBN 10: 0-8163-2383-6 (pbk.)

10 11 12 13 14 • 5 4 3 2

Soups, Salads & Sandwiches

With the Micheff Sisters

A Vegan Vegetarian Cookbook

3ABN BOOKS

P.O. Box 220, West Frankfort, Illinois
www.3ABN.org

Pacific Press® Publishing Association
Nampa, Idaho
Oshawa, Ontario, Canada
www.pacificpress.com

Foreword

As we look back over our childhood, we can't help but feel the blessings that come from having Christian parents. Our home was always filled with neighbors, friends, and church family just getting together around our table for some of Mom's delicious soups, stews, or sandwiches. To this day, Dad doesn't think it's a meal without a sandwich! Although Mom never published a cookbook, people frequently asked for her recipes to learn how to make such wonderful tasting "healthy" food.

We can't remember a time when our sisters were not in the kitchen with Mom. Although, sometimes we smile when we think back on those early years! Not all their creations were successes! Being the "little brothers," we were the "official testers," and we can confirm that some recipes had us asking for seconds while others were, well—let's just say, "less than wonderful"! Happily, they kept trying and now have more successes than failures!

We're sure Mom never dreamed at how much God would bless her efforts to teach our sisters how to cook. Today they're sharing their recipes with people all over the world. We're proud of all that God has accomplished through them, but what we love most about our sisters is their love for Jesus and their service for others.

We hope this cookbook will encourage you in your journey to better health, and you can take it from us, eating healthy never tasted so good!

With our blessings and prayers,

the Micheff brothers,
Jim and Ken

Tribute to Dad

When we hear the word *Daddy,* our thoughts are filled with warm and treasured memories. Some of the mental pictures we love to remember about our precious father are his early morning praises to Jesus. Even though he couldn't keep in tune, we loved hearing Daddy sing loudly to wake us each morning, "There is Sunshine in My Soul Today" and "Oh, How I Love Jesus." We also loved sitting around our dining room table, listening to him tell stories of his childhood, which often produced squeals of laughter.

Daddy could always think of something fun to do, especially if it involved work! And there was never a dull moment in our home. When we got older, he wanted to be sure we learned how to be responsible, so he bought some baby calves for us to care for. Those early morning feeding times and cleaning out the "honey" (not the kind you cook with!) in the barn taught us more than we realized at the time. Dad's sense of humor was amazing!

One night as we were cleaning out the barn and taking care of our calves, some guys from the academy showed up to see us. We were mortified to be seen in our grubby clothes with hairnets on our heads! With a sly smile, Dad handed the guys a pitchfork and under his watchful eye they made fast work of our barn job! Now as we look back over our lives, we are so thankful that God gave us a Christian father who was not only determined to raise his children to know and love the Lord Jesus Christ, but to teach us how to be responsible, and to work hard. Today, all five of his children are serving the Lord in full-time ministry.

Daddy, we all know how much you love soups and sandwiches, yes, even for special holiday meals! Throughout the years, we have enjoyed your own creative recipes and we can testify—they were and still are, amazingly delicious! You are the inspiration behind this cookbook and just like you have always shared with us, we count it a privilege to share our recipes with others.

We want you to know that we embrace the values that you have set before us and we join you in your prayer that someday soon we will all be together in heaven. With all our love, we dedicate this cookbook to you. We thank you for your prayers of blessing that it will be a stepping-stone to better health for all. May God continue to bless your prayer ministry and all you do for Jesus.

We love you, Daddy,
Your daughters,
Linda, Brenda, and Cinda

Acknowledgments

We would like to express our heartfelt thanks to all those who helped make
Soups, Salads & Sandwiches With the Micheff Sisters possible:

James & Bernice Micheff

Ken & Tammy Micheff

Jim & Gail Micheff

Crystal Micheff

Jenny Trubey

Joel Sanner

Catie & David Sanner

Jim Johnson

Tim Walsh

Vic & Carol Guajardo

Harley & Kay Wold

Bill & Lin Kiser

Virginia Pfeifle

Willie & Jodi Iwankiw

Julie Iwankiw

Rick & Valerie DeFluiter

Jacob DeFluiter

Corrine Jones

Martha Pleshka

George Whiteaker

Galen & Mickey Miller

Sandy Lee

Chrystique Neibauer

Mellisa Hoffman

Kay Kuzma

Table of Contents

Introduction

As we look back over the years, we can see how God has continually blessed us with new and better ways to prepare healthy meals for our families. Learning to enjoy the variety of foods in their simplicity has been a delightful experience for us! And really it does not get much simpler than soup, salads, and sandwiches. Yet they are so delicious *and* nutritious!

Growing up we all looked forward to Mom's homemade soup and Dad's scrumptious sandwiches! After a long walk from school, it was like rolling out a welcome mat when the smells of food cooking on the stove greeted us at the door. It set the mood for a happy and peaceful home. Isn't it wonderful how God uses the little things in life to make us feel loved and blessed?

In this cookbook we share with you delicious soups, stews, and chilies along with mouthwatering salads, sandwiches, and a special section on Crock-Pot cooking. With life so busy and yes, even crazy at times, Crock-Pot cooking takes the stress out of preparing meals in a hurry. We pray you will be blessed as you try these simple and tasty recipes.

God in His great love for us has created everything needed for a healthy mind, body, and spirit that we may all grow and prosper in good health. And even though our Lord is daily providing for all our needs here on earth, He is even now preparing something even greater for us in heaven. We believe that Jesus is preparing a special banquet for all those who love Him and serve Him. What a welcome mat that will be when the wonderful smells coming from the heavenly kitchen greet us as we walk through those pearly gates! As our eyes feast on the luscious and delicious foods the Master Chef has prepared for us, we will be overwhelmed with joy, peace, and love! We look forward to sharing that special meal with you and all your loved ones!

May you be blessed as you try these appetizing recipes and look forward with anticipation to all that God has in store for those who love Him!

With God's Richest Blessings!
Linda, Brenda, and Cinda

Soups

Asparagus Soup
p. 22

Ball Park Soup
p. 13

Tuscan Four
Bean Soup
p. 29

Hamburger
Pasta Soup
p. 30

Potato Leek Soup
p. 16

Zesty Red
Lentil Soup
p. 26

Home Style Vegetable Soup

4 cups shredded cabbage

2 cups sliced carrots

1 cup diced onions

3 cups diced potatoes

10 cups water

3 tablespoons McKay's Chicken Seasoning (Vegan Special)

1 tablespoon dried parsley

1 teaspoon onion powder

2 teaspoons low sodium salt

Put all ingredients in a large kettle and cook until vegetables are done, approximately 20 to 25 minutes. Turn down to simmer for an additional 15 to 20 minutes. Serve hot with your favorite salad, dinner rolls, and jam. Enjoy!

My mother-in-law Aggie is a wonderful cook and has cooked at several youth camps and camp meetings. She has a special gift for flavoring foods. This soup is a spin off one of her recipes that is a favorite of my husband. They both gave this version two thumbs up! —Linda

Yield: 10 cups

(1/2 cup) Calories 25 Total Fat 0g Saturated Fat 0g Sodium 377.9mg Total Carbohydrates 5.7g Fiber 1.0g Protein 0.63g

Ball Park Soup

In large soup pot, combine all ingredients except for pasta. Cook approximately 30 minutes on medium-low heat (just a slow simmer) or until vegetables are tender. Increase heat to maintain a rapid boil and add pasta. Cook approximately 5 minutes or until pasta is tender but not too soft (*al denté*). Serve hot.

This soup is sure to be a "home run" with your friends and family! It is a simple soup with a traditional tasting beefy broth. I love easy soup recipes that I can simmer on my back burner so I can multitask and get lots of other work done while it is cooking! To complete your meal, add some whole grain buns and a salad and you are sure to hit it "out of the park"! —Brenda

1 medium onion, diced

1 cup vegetable stock

8 cups water

2 beef-flavored vegan bouillon cubes

2 cups shredded cabbage

1 cup sliced carrots

3 cups diced potatoes

1 cup sliced vegetarian hot dogs

1 teaspoon onion powder

1 cup pasta noodles

Yield: 8 cups

(1/2 cup) Calories 57 Total Fat 0.4g Saturated Fat 0g Sodium 256.2mg Total Carbohydrates 10.7g Fiber 1.1g Protein 2.8g

Old Fashioned Vegetable Soup

8 cups water

1 quart tomatoes

1 cup diced celery

2 medium onions, diced

1/2 cup quick barley

3 teaspoons McKay's Chicken Seasoning (Vegan Special)

1 teaspoon dried or fresh parsley

1 teaspoon sea salt

1 teaspoon onion powder

1 1/4 teaspoons celery salt

1/2 teaspoon chili powder

1/2 teaspoon garlic powder

1/2 cup diced potatoes

2 cups frozen mixed vegetables

1/4 cup alphabet pasta

In a large stockpot, combine all ingredients except the pasta and bring to a boil. Adjust heat to maintain a slow simmer. Cook approximately 1 hour until all vegetables are tender and then add the pasta. Continue cooking only until pasta is tender, not mushy. Serve hot.

This is such a quick and easy soup recipe. I love recipes that let me just dump everything in the pot. I wasn't intentionally trying to imitate any soup but all my test tasters made the comment that this soup tastes very similar to Campbell's Vegetable Soup! Be careful not to cook the pasta too much because the tiny alphabet pasta soaks up juices even after being removed from heat.
—Brenda

Yield: 12 cups

(1/2 cup) Calories 60   Total Fat 0.3g   Saturated Fat 0g   Sodium 273.9mg   Total Carbohydrates 13.5g   Fiber 3.2g   Protein 2.36g

French Onion Soup

Heat oil in large stockpot over medium heat. Sauté slivered onion until clear. Add all other ingredients and simmer on low for one hour. Fifteen minutes before serving, place bread on baking sheet. Brush tops of bread with olive oil and sprinkle with Parmesan cheese. Place under oven broiler until golden. Ladle onion soup into individual bowls and place one slice of toasted bread on top. Serve hot.

My husband loves French onion soup but the typical recipe is not very healthy. All that melted cheese just isn't good for him, so I came up with this recipe! He is such a finicky eater that if I can please him, I know I have a winner! He gave me the "two thumbs up," which is the best stamp of approval I could ask for! I don't think you will even miss all that cheese! —Brenda

1 tablespoon canola oil

2 medium onions, slivered

2 cloves garlic, minced

1 cup vegetable stock

5 cups water

2 1/2 tablespoons vegetable bouillon

6 slices French bread

2 tablespoons olive oil

1/4 cup vegan Parmesan cheese

Yield: 6 cups

(1/2 cup) Calories 99 Total Fat 4.8g Saturated Fat 0.5g Sodium 176mg Total Carbohydrates 11g Fiber 0.8g Protein 3.3g

Potato Leek Soup

2 tablespoons soy margarine

2 cups chopped leeks, rinsed well and drained

1 medium onion, diced

1/2 cup diced celery

4 cups diced potatoes

4 cups Imagine Organic No-Chicken Broth, or vegetable broth of your choice

2 cups water

2 tablespoons McKay's Chicken Seasoning (Vegan Special)

1 tablespoon parsley

1 teaspoon celery salt

1/2 teaspoon thyme

1 cup original flavor Silk Creamer

Heat margarine in large stockpot over medium heat. Sauté onion and leeks until clear. Add all other ingredients except for Silk Creamer. Cook for one hour until potatoes are tender. Remove three cups of soup and pour into blender. Process until smooth and then return to rest of soup. Add Silk Creamer and cook another five minutes. Serve hot!

This is a creamy soup with a wonderful balance of leeks and potatoes. I love potatoes in just about everything, so this is definitely one of my favorites. Omit the leeks and add a can of creamed corn and it instantly becomes a potato corn chowder. Serve with some crusty European-style bread. —Brenda

Yield: 8 cups

(1/2 cup) Calories 59 Total Fat 2.5g Saturated Fat 0.5g Sodium 449.9mg Total Carbohydrates 8.4g Fiber 0.8g Protein 0.9g

Carrot Ginger Bisque

Heat margarine in large stockpot over medium heat. Sauté diced onion until clear. Add celery, carrots, and sweet potatoes and cook until tender. Remove from heat and add all other ingredients, except creamer. Process two cups at a time in blender until smooth. Return blended soup to stockpot. Bring to a boil and then adjust heat to simmer for one hour. Add Silk Creamer and simmer another 15 minutes. Serve hot.

My friend, Bobby Davis, inspired this soup. He ordered carrot soup at a restaurant and loved it so much he asked if I would come up with a recipe for it! It took several attempts before I discovered just the right blend of ingredients. I served this to friends who don't even like carrots, and they loved this soup. If you love the fresh taste of ginger, increase the amount to one tablespoon. Be careful, though; too much can easily overpower the recipe.
—Brenda

2 tablespoons soy margarine

1 medium onion, diced

1 cup diced celery

3 cups sliced carrots

1 cup diced sweet potato

2 teaspoons grated fresh ginger

4 cups carrot juice

3 tablespoons McKay's Chicken Seasoning (Vegan Special)

2 teaspoons sugar

1/2 teaspoon celery salt

1/2 cup coconut milk

2 tablespoons peanut butter (smooth)

2 tablespoons lemon juice

1 tablespoon honey

Pinch salt

1 cup original flavor Silk Creamer

Yield: 6 cups

(1/2 cup) Calories 166 Total Fat 8.1g Saturated Fat 3.1g Sodium 573.2mg Total Carbohydrates 21.4g Fiber 2.5g Protein 2.9g

Southern Split Pea Soup

2 cups dried split peas, rinsed well

6 cups water

1 medium onion, diced

2 vegetable bouillon cubes

1/2 cup diced carrots

1 teaspoon sea salt

In a large stockpot, combine all ingredients. Bring to a boil, and then adjust heat to maintain a slow simmer. Cook for 1 to 2 hours until peas have completely dissolved into a thick soup. Serve hot.

It sure doesn't get easier than this! You can also put these ingredients in your Crock-Pot in the morning on low. When you return home, supper is ready! My mom told me that of all my soups, this one was her favorite. Now that is one recommendation I treasure. —Brenda

Yield: 8 cups

(1/2 cup) Calories 92 Total Fat 0.6g Saturated Fat 0g Sodium 142.2mg Total Carbohydrates 16g Fiber 6.5g Protein 6.4g

Mashed Potato Soup

Puree the onions with one cup of the water in a blender. Put all the ingredients except for the mashed potatoes and sour cream in a medium-sized kettle. Cook for approximately 15 minutes until celery is done. Add soy milk and mix the instant mashed potatoes into the kettle, stirring constantly until well blended. Cook 3 to 4 minutes. Remove from heat and mix in the Tofutti Sour Supreme. Serve hot.

This yummy soup was inspired by my need to come up with a meal in a hurry! It will go even faster if the celery and carrots are cooked in the microwave and added to the soup after they are tender. Sometimes I make this soup when I am looking for something to take to my 94-year-old friend that she will like. Dorothy loves potato soup and I love the smile on her face when I share some with her. I have found that it is really the simple things in life that bring the most joy. —Linda

1 + 5 cups water

1 cup diced onions

1/2 cup diced celery

1/2 cup shredded carrots

1/4 cup thinly sliced green onions and stems

2 teaspoons low sodium salt

1/2 teaspoon celery salt

1 1/2 teaspoons seasoned salt

1/2 teaspoon onion powder

1 cup plain soy milk

1 3/4 cups instant mashed potato mix

1 cup Tofutti Sour Supreme

Yield: 8 cups

(1/2 cup) Calories 72 Total Fat 2.7g Saturated Fat 1g Sodium 422.6mg Total Carbohydrates 11.2g Fiber 0.7g Protein 1.3g

Broccoli Rice Soup

1 tablespoon extra virgin olive oil

1 tablespoon soy margarine

1 medium onion, diced

1 large leek, diced

1 cup peeled and diced carrot

1 large head of broccoli, chopped (approximately 8 cups)

1/2 cup medium grain brown rice

5 cups water

2 tablespoons McKay's Chicken Seasoning (Vegan Special)

2 bay leaves

1 8-ounce package Tofutti Better Than Cream Cheese

Salt to taste

Carrot curls for garnish

Paprika for garnish

Heat the soy margarine and olive oil in a large stockpot over medium heat. Stirring frequently to avoid burning, sauté the onion, leek, and carrots until the onion is soft and clear.

Divide the broccoli into small florets and cut off the stems. Peel the large stems. Chop all broccoli into small pieces. Add the broccoli, rice, water, McKay's Chicken Seasoning (Vegan Special), and leaves, into the stockpot. Bring to a boil and reduce heat to low. Cover and simmer until the rice is tender. Remove the bay leaves and stir in the Better Than Cream Cheese. Keep stirring until the cream cheese is melted and well mixed in the soup. Salt to taste. Garnish with carrot curls and a sprinkle of paprika.

I like to put this soup in a large thermos and take on picnics or send in school lunches. It is thick and hearty and guaranteed to keep you feeling full and satisfied for hours! —Cinda

Yield: 10 cups

(1/2 cup) Calories 80 Total Fat 3.4g Saturated Fat 1.1g Sodium 248.1mg Total Carbohydrates 11.1g Fiber 0.5g Protein 1.8g

Creamy Corn Soup

Remove kernels from corn and set aside. Put the water, vegetables (except the corn), and seasoning in a medium kettle and bring to a boil. Turn the heat down to a low boil. Cook for 10 minutes. Add the corn. Cook until all vegetables are tender, approximately 20 minutes. Put three cups of the corn soup in the blender and blend until smooth. Pour back into kettle. Take the soup off of heat and stir in the Tofutti Sour Supreme until it is well blended. Garnish with fresh chives. Serve hot with your favorite whole wheat bread, spreads, and a garden salad.

Fresh sweet corn is always a treat in our family. When we can't get fresh corn, then I use the corn I freeze in the summer for this recipe. My husband loves just about any kind of soup. I love how the rich flavors simmering in the kettle on the stove fill our home with a rich, inviting aroma! It doesn't get much better than homemade bread and a big pot of soup to make my family feel special. It always fills my heart with joy when I see the smiles on my family and friends enjoying a bowl of soup around our table. —Linda

3 cups uncooked sweet corn, freshly cut off cob

6 cups water

1/4 cup shredded carrots

1/2 cup diced onions

1/2 cup chopped celery

1/2 teaspoon ground celery seeds

1 teaspoon low sodium salt

1 teaspoon seasoned salt

1 teaspoon onion powder

1/2 cup Tofutti Sour Supreme

1/4 cup fresh chives for garnish

Yield: 5 cups

(1/2 cup) Calories 81 Total Fat 2.6g Saturated Fat 0.9g Sodium 333.7mg Total Carbohydrates 14g Fiber 1.6g Protein 2.1g

Asparagus Soup

5 cups young asparagus

2 + 1 tablespoons soy margarine

1 medium onion, minced

3 tablespoons flour

3 cups vegetable stock

2 teaspoons McKay's Chicken Seasoning (Vegan Special)

Salt to taste

1 1/2 cups original flavor Silk Creamer

Diced fresh or dried chervil for garnish

Wash asparagus and break off the ends. Cut the tips off the asparagus and set aside. Cut the remaining spears into 1-inch pieces. Melt 2 tablespoons soy margarine in a medium stockpot. Sauté the onion on medium heat until translucent, stirring often to avoid burning. Add the asparagus (not the tips) and sauté about 3 minutes. Stir in the flour and cook for 1 minute. Stir in the vegetable stock and McKay's Chicken Seasoning (Vegan Special) and season with salt. Bring to a boil and then reduce heat and simmer for 15 to 20 minutes, until asparagus is tender. Remove from heat and, using a hand blender, blend until thoroughly processed and smooth. (You can also use a food processor or regular blender.) Add the soy creamer. Heat on low until hot. In a small saucepan, melt 1 tablespoon soy margarine. Sauté the asparagus tips for 2 to 3 minutes, until tender crisp. Add to the soup. Serve with the chervil sprinkled over the top.

Asparagus brings fond memories of my childhood to mind. We were very poor, yet our mother was determined that she was going to feed her family as healthfully as possible. We would drive down country roads looking for wild asparagus growing beside the road. She could prepare and season it so that we all loved it—even Daddy! When my son David was little, he would always ask Nana for her asparagus—and still loves it today. My husband loves this soup thickened a little more and served over toast. —Cinda

Yield: 6 cups

(1/2 cup) Calories 84 Total Fat 5.3g Saturated Fat 1g Sodium 175.3mg Total Carbohydrates 7g Fiber 1.3g Protein 1.8g

Roasted Red Pepper Soup

In a medium saucepan, sauté onion in the olive oil until clear. Add the potato, garlic, bay leaves, and marjoram. Sauté over medium heat, stirring often, until the mixture begins to brown. Stir in the tomato paste, peppers, paprika, salt, and vegetable stock. Bring to a boil, then lower heat and simmer with cover on for 25 minutes. Remove the bay leaves and with hand blender, blend until smooth, or blend in a food processor or regular blender two cups at a time. Garnish with a sprig of fresh marjoram.

I love to serve this in small soup cups with homemade corn bread or polenta croutons, along with a sprig of fresh marjoram. The presentation is beautiful and makes a wonderful addition to a brunch or luncheon. Of course, it is also good served for a light lunch or supper. —Cinda

2 tablespoons extra virgin olive oil

1 medium sweet onion, diced

2 small potatoes, peeled and thinly sliced

2 garlic cloves, minced

2 bay leaves

1 1/2 tablespoons dried marjoram

1 tablespoon tomato paste

4 to 5 large red bell peppers, roasted and coarsely diced, or 14-ounce jar roasted red peppers

1 1/2 teaspoons sweet paprika

Salt to taste

4 cups basic vegetable stock

Fresh marjoram for garnish

Yield: 5 cups

(1/2 cup) Calories 82 Total Fat 3.7g Saturated Fat 0.4g Sodium 57.1mg Total Carbohydrates 11.3g Fiber 2g Protein 2.3g

Mexican Corn Chowder

1 tablespoon soy margarine

1 medium onion, diced

1/2 cup diced celery

2 tablespoons diced red
bell pepper

1 tablespoon diced
jalapeño peppers

1/2 cup diced green chiles

1 teaspoon celery salt

1 tablespoon McKay's
Chicken Seasoning
(Vegan Special)

1 teaspoon chili powder

3 cups creamed corn

2 tablespoons sugar

1 teaspoon parsley

1 cup cold original flavor
Silk Creamer

2 tablespoons cornstarch

Heat margarine in a large saucepan over medium heat. Sauté onion in margarine until clear. Add celery and red pepper. When pepper is tender, add all other ingredients except the Silk Creamer and cornstarch. Simmer on low for one hour. Mix together cold Silk Creamer and cornstarch and add to soup. Cook an additional 15 minutes until slightly thickened. Serve hot.

This is a spicy twist to the typical corn chowder recipe. If you want to kick it up a notch, add extra jalapeño peppers. If you want a more traditional chowder, just omit the red pepper, chiles, and jalapeño. But I highly recommend that you try this recipe as it is first—you might not want to change a thing. Believe it or not, I serve it with my homemade corn bread. Nope! Not too much corn for me. —Brenda

Yield: 10 cups

(1/2 cup) Calories 58   Total Fat 1.6g   Saturated Fat 0.2g   Sodium 194.6mg   Total Carbohydrates 11.3g   Fiber 0.7g   Protein 0.8g

Eggless Drop Soup

Put all the ingredients in a medium-sized kettle. Cook at a low boil 20 minutes; reduce heat to simmer and cook 10 minutes more. Serve hot with your favorite oriental meal.

I purchase Light Gluten Shreds from Creative Cuisine. (For information on this product, check the Resources section on page 143.) These dehydrated gluten shreds have an egglike texture when cooked in the soup. Serve this tasty soup with your favorite oriental meal. Enjoy! —Linda

4 cups water

3 tablespoons McKay's Chicken Seasoning (Vegan Special)

1 cup Light Gluten Shreds

1/2 cup minced fresh spinach

1/4 cup sliced green onions

1 tablespoon nutritional yeast flakes

1 teaspoon minced fresh garlic

Yield: 4 cups

(1/2 cup) Calories 35 Total Fat 0g Saturated Fat 0g Sodium 646.6mg Total Carbohydrates 4.7g Fiber 0.9g Protein 5.2g

Zesty Red Lentil Soup

1 1/2 cups dried red lentils

2 1/2 cups no salt
  added canned diced
  tomatoes

1 cup mild salsa

2 cups plain, no salt added
  tomato sauce

7 cups water

1 tablespoon minced fresh
  garlic

1/2 cup sliced green
  onions

1/2 cup minced onions

2 teaspoons low sodium
  salt

1/2 teaspoon seasoned salt

1 teaspoon onion powder

1/2 teaspoon dried or
  coarsely chopped
  fresh basil

1 cup diced zucchini

1 cup diced summer
  yellow squash

2 cups chopped fresh
  spinach

1/2 cup diced red bell
  pepper

Pick through the lentils to remove any debris and then rinse thoroughly. In a large kettle add all the ingredients, except the zucchini, summer squash, spinach, and red bell pepper. Heat to a slow boil on medium-high heat. Continue cooking at a slow boil approximately 35 minutes or until lentils are tender. Add the summer squash, zucchini, spinach, and red bell pepper and simmer for another 5 minutes. Serve with your favorite vegetable salad and whole grain bread.

This lentil soup is not only full of good nutrition, but it is so good! In my opinion, there is nothing that can compare to a hot bowl of soup on a cold evening that is shared together as a family. Times spent together around the table make for lasting memories. —Linda

Yield: 13 cups

(1/2 cup) Calories 58 Total Fat 0.2g Saturated Fat 0g Sodium 159.1mg Total Carbohydrates 10.8g Fiber 4.4g Protein 3.9g

Italian White Bean Soup

In a large stockpot, heat olive oil. Sauté onion and celery until onion is clear. Stir frequently to avoid burning. Add the rest of the ingredients and simmer on low for 20 to 25 minutes. Remove from heat. Put two cups of the soup into a blender. Blend and then return the blended soup to the pot. Add the fresh spinach and stir well.

Our mom used to make bean soup quite frequently when we were growing up, and I have always loved it. Beans are so good for you, and the spinach gives this soup added nutrition. It is a little different than the one Mom used to make, but I think you will love it. —Cinda

1 tablespoon extra virgin olive oil

1 medium onion, diced

1 cup diced celery

1 clove garlic, minced

2 16-ounce cans no salt added white kidney beans, drained

3 1/2 cups water

2 tablespoons McKay's Chicken Seasoning (Vegan Special)

1/4 teaspoon dried thyme

4 cups coarsely chopped fresh spinach

3/4 teaspoon Vege-Sal

Yield: 5 cups

(1/2 cup) Calories 263 Total Fat 2g Saturated Fat 0.4g Sodium 469mg Total Carbohydrates 46g Fiber 11.4g Protein 17g

Country Tomato & Bread Soup

2 tablespoons extra virgin olive oil

1 medium onion, minced

1 teaspoon crushed red pepper flakes (use less if you don't want it spicy)

3/4 cup coarsely chopped fresh basil leaves

2 cloves garlic, minced

1 teaspoon dried oregano

2 28-ounce cans no salt added whole tomatoes

4 cups vegetable stock

1 loaf Italian bread

Heat olive oil in a large stockpot and sauté onion until clear. Add the spices and sauté one minute more, stirring so they do not burn.

Crush tomatoes and add to stockpot, including all the juices. Add the vegetable stock and bring to a boil. Reduce heat and simmer for 15 to 20 minutes. Remove from heat and puree, either with a hand blender, or transfer to a food processor or regular blender. Break the bread into small chunks. Pour the hot soup into individual serving bowls and put a handful of the bread on top. Serve immediately.

I love to serve this soup with a spoonful of homemade pesto drizzled over the bread. It reminds me of a warm evening in the Tuscan countryside. Make sure you don't add the bread until right before you eat, as it soaks up all of the soup if it sits too long. It will still taste good—just more like a tomato bread pudding. —Cinda

Yield: 14 cups

(1/2 cup) Calories 65 Total Fat 1.7g Saturated Fat 0.2g Sodium 116.4mg Total Carbohydrates 11g Fiber 1.4g Protein 2g

Tuscan Four Bean Soup

Heat oil over medium-low heat in a large soup pot. Add onions, celery, and carrots. Sauté until onions are clear. Stir often to avoid burning. Add the rest of the ingredients and simmer on low for 15 to 20 minutes. Using a hand-held blender for just a few seconds, puree coarsely. If you do not have a hand-held blender, put 2 to 3 cups of soup in a blender or food processor, cover, and puree coarsely. Return the pureed soup back into the pot. Stir well. Garnish with some fresh herbs.

I guess you could say that I pretty much love anything Italian! Italy is one of my favorite countries to visit, and I love trying their simple yet flavorful foods. This soup is just that, simple to make and full of flavor. Dip a piece of fresh Italian bread in this soup and picture yourself dining alfresco in their beautiful countryside! —Cinda

2 medium onions, diced

2 tablespoons extra virgin olive oil

1 teaspoon dried oregano

3/4 cup coarsely chopped fresh basil leaves

2 large carrots, peeled and diced

3 large celery stalks, diced

4 cups water

4 tablespoons McKay's Chicken Seasoning (Vegan Special)

1 28-ounce can no salt added crushed tomatoes

1 15 1/2-ounce can no salt added dark red kidney beans, drained

1 15 1/2-ounce can no salt added pinto beans, drained

1 15 1/2-ounce can no salt added garbanzo beans, drained

1 15 1/2-ounce can no salt added navy beans, drained

Fresh herbs for garnish

Yield: 14 cups

(1/2 cup) Calories 89 Total Fat 1.4g Saturated Fat 0.2g Sodium 257.2mg Total Carbohydrates 15.5g Fiber 4.8g Protein 4.3g

Hamburger Pasta Soup

1 tablespoon extra virgin olive oil

1 cup diced onions

2 tablespoons minced fresh garlic

1 cup diced red bell pepper

1 1-pound 4-ounce can Worthington burger or 3 cups vegetarian burger of your choice

8 cups water

4 cups diced canned tomatoes

2 1/2 cups garlic herb spaghetti sauce

2 cups cut fresh green beans

2 cups diced yellow summer squash

2 cups diced zucchini

4 tablespoons McKay's Beef Seasoning (Vegan Special)

1 teaspoon ground oregano

1 teaspoon onion powder

1/2 teaspoon fresh or dried basil

2 cups cooked small pasta shells

Heat olive oil in a large skillet on medium high heat. Sauté the onions, garlic, red pepper, and vegetarian burger until onions are clear. In a large kettle put the water, canned tomatoes, garlic herb spaghetti sauce, green beans, yellow squash, zucchini, and seasonings. Cook until the green beans are almost done. Add the small shell pasta and burger mixture. Cook until pasta is done. Cool slightly and serve.

There is something so down home about a pot of soup served with homemade bread. I love to invite my friends over and share this simple but delicious meal together. It is a wonderful bonding time. We love spending time with our family and friends! —Linda

Yield: 20 cups

(1/2 cup) Calories 50 Total Fat 0.7g Saturated Fat 0.1g Sodium 263.8mg Total Carbohydrates 7.8g Fiber 1.7g Protein 3.7g

Stews

African
Peanut Stew
p. 49

Mandarin
Beef Stew
p. 46

Bangkok Stew
p. 47

Irish Stew
With Dumplings
p. 43

Summer
Vegetable Stew
p. 34

Latino Black
Bean Stew
p. 44

Summer Vegetable Stew

2 tablespoons olive oil

1 medium onion, diced

1 cup slivered red bell
    pepper

1 tablespoon sliced fresh
    jalapeño

1 teaspoon minced fresh
    garlic

1 teaspoon onion powder

1 teaspoon dried dill

1 teaspoon low sodium
    salt

1 tablespoon McKay's
    Chicken Seasoning
    (Vegan Special)

2 cups diced zucchini

1 cup sliced yellow
    summer squash

2 cups diced eggplant

1/2 cup sliced
    mushrooms

4 cups no salt added
    canned diced
    tomatoes

3/4 cup sweet corn,
    freshly cut off cob

1 cup medium-diced
    gluten (your favorite)

1 cup small broccoli
    florets

1 cup small cauliflower
    florets

Heat the olive oil in a large kettle over medium heat. Sauté the onion, pepper, jalapeño, fresh garlic, and seasonings in olive oil until tender. Add the rest of the ingredients and simmer for about 15 minutes until all the vegetables are crunchy tender.

In my opinion, Mom is the greatest cook on this planet. Over the years she has made her kitchen a place where family and friends love to linger. Whenever we come home we are greeted with delicious smells of home baked bread, stews, or soups. The foods that she has prepared over the years have become a precious heirloom not only to me, but to my sisters and brothers as well. Mom inspired this simple but scrumptious stew. I love the rich flavors that come from blending the different vegetables. Make up a batch and enjoy! —Linda

Yield: 10 cups

(1/2 cup) Calories 43 Total Fat 1.6g Saturated Fat 0.2g Sodium 176.4mg Total Carbohydrates 6.7g Fiber 1.9g Protein 1.8g

Stroganoff Stew

Heat the oil in a medium-sized skillet over medium heat. Sauté the onions until almost clear, and then add the mushrooms, sausage crumbles, and seasonings. Set aside. In a medium-sized kettle put 3 1/2 cups of soy milk. Take 1/2 cup of cold soy milk and mix with 1/2 cup of unbleached flour and melted soy margarine. Whip together until smooth and stir into the cold soy milk in the kettle. Turn on the heat to medium high and stir until it bubbles and thickens slightly. Add the sausage mixture and soy noodles into the white sauce and stir gently until thoroughly mixed. Serve with raw vegetables and whole grain bread.

I served this delicious stew to my taste testers Dad, Mom, Chrystique Neibauer, and Mellisa Hoffen. They liked it so much they took some home for Mellisa's mom to try. But when Dad gave it the thumbs up, I knew this recipe was ready for the cookbook! Hope you enjoy it too! —Linda

1 tablespoon canola oil

1/2 cup diced onions

1/2 cup sliced fresh green onions

1 cup sliced mushrooms

2 cups Morning Star Sausage Crumbles or vegetarian burger of your choice

1 1/2 teaspoons low sodium salt

1 teaspoon McKay's Beef Seasoning (Vegan Special)

1 teaspoon McKay's Chicken Seasoning (Vegan Special)

3 1/2 + 1/2 cups soy milk

1/4 cup soy margarine, melted

1/2 cup unbleached white flour

4 cups cooked soy noodles

Yield: 8 cups

(1/2 cup) Calories 211 Total Fat 5.9g Saturated Fat 1.5g Sodium 291.3mg Total Carbohydrates 35.9g Fiber 2.3g Protein 3.8g

Chunky Chicken Stew

2 cups diced Cedar Lake Vege-Chik'n frozen roll

1 tablespoon canola oil

1 cup slivered onion

1 teaspoon minced fresh garlic

1 cup chopped red bell pepper

2 cups small broccoli florets

1 cup small cauliflower florets

1 1/2 cups slivered celery

1 cup sliced carrots

3 1/2 + 1/2 cups plain soy milk

1/2 cup unbleached flour

1/4 cup melted soy margarine

1 teaspoon McKay's Chicken Seasoning (Vegan Special)

2 teaspoons low sodium salt

Remove chicken roll from freezer and thaw overnight in refrigerator. Dice. In a large skillet on medium-high heat add the canola oil and sauté the onions. Add the garlic and red pepper and cook until tender. Cook the broccoli, cauliflower, celery, and carrots in the microwave for about 6 minutes. In a medium-sized kettle put 3 1/2 cups of cold soy milk. Take remaining 1/2 cup of the soy milk and stir in 1/2 cup unbleached flour and 1/4 cup melted soy margarine. Whip together until creamy with no lumps and stir into cold soy milk in the kettle. Add the seasonings and bring to a soft boil stirring constantly until thickened. Add remaining ingredients and cook until hot.

Serve with homemade bread and a relish tray. Sometimes I double this recipe so that I can have enough left over to make potpie for another meal. Just put the leftover stew in a baking dish and top with your favorite biscuits or piecrust. Bake at 350 degrees for about 20 minutes until crust or biscuits are done and stew is hot and bubbly. I have found out that planning ahead for the week gives me lots more time to accomplish some of the other things I need to do. So make some extra stew and take time to smell the roses! —Linda

Yield: 8 cups

(1/2 cup) Calories 129   Total Fat 9g   Saturated Fat 2.2g   Sodium 428.8mg   Total Carbohydrates 6.7g   Fiber 0.9g   Protein 6.3g

Gnocchi Vegetable Stew

In a large stockpot sauté onion until clear over medium heat, stirring to avoid burning. Add the leek, celery, and carrots and continue to sauté for 3 minutes more. Mix the broth together in a separate bowl and then add to the sautéed vegetables. Stir, and then add the zucchini, yellow squash, butternut squash, white potatoes, and fresh green beans. Bring to a boil, then reduce heat, cover, and simmer on medium-low for 30 minutes. Add the broccoli, gnocchi, and edamame and stir. Continue to cook for 10 more minutes uncovered. Serve hot.

My daughter Catie and I love gnocchi! We fell in love with the little homemade potato dumplings when we were in Italy, and ordered them with every meal we had while we were there. They are a perfect addition to this hearty and nutrition-packed stew. If there are any leftovers, I make a potpie with them. —Cinda

1 large onion, diced

1 cup diced leeks

1 cup diced celery

1 cup diced carrots

2 cups cubed zucchini

2 cups cubed yellow squash

3 cups cubed butternut squash

3 cups cubed white potatoes

3 cups cut fresh green beans

3 cups broccoli florets

2 cups potato gnocchi

1 16-ounce bag frozen edamame

Broth (recipe below)

BROTH

6 cups vegetable broth

3/4 cup flour

1/4 cup Bragg Liquid Aminos

1 teaspoon sea salt

2 tablespoons McKay's Beef Seasoning (Vegan Special)

1 tablespoon Vegex brewers yeast extract

Yield: 20 cups

(1/2 cup) Calories 55 Total Fat 1g Saturated Fat 0.1g Sodium 269.8mg Total Carbohydrates 9.9g Fiber 1.5g Protein 2.1g

Lumberjack Stew

1 tablespoon oil

1 medium onion, diced

2 cloves garlic, minced

1 cup diced celery

1 cup gluten of your choice

2 cups sliced carrots

3 cups cubed potatoes

6 cups water

3 tablespoons vegetarian beef-style bouillon

1 1/2 cups cut green beans

1 cup instant mashed potatoes

Heat oil in a large stockpot. Sauté onion in oil until clear. Add garlic, celery, and gluten. When celery is tender add water, bouillon, carrots, and green beans. Bring to a boil, and then adjust heat to maintain a slow simmer for 45 minutes. Add potatoes and continue cooking another 15 minutes until potatoes are tender. Add instant mashed potatoes and cook another 5 minutes until stew is slightly thickened.

I don't know anyone who loves soups and stews more than our dad, so, of course, when I created this recipe, I asked him to taste it for me. He gave it 4 stars and even gave it this name. He said it was hearty and filling enough for hard-working lumberjacks! That was good enough for me. Thanks, Dad.
—Brenda

Yield: 12 cups

(1/2 cup) Calories 36 Total Fat 0.7g Saturated Fat 0.1g Sodium 198.8mg Total Carbohydrates 6.2g Fiber 1g Protein 1.2g

Italian Sausage Stew

Put all the ingredients, except for the cooked pasta, in a medium-sized kettle. Cook on medium-high heat for about 20 minutes until vegetables are tender. Add the cooked pasta and serve with your favorite salad, bread, and healthy dessert.

This is a spin off of one of our childhood dishes. Sometimes we would make it with only canned tomatoes and macaroni—one of my favorite dishes! When it was my time to cook the family meal, I always made tomato and macaroni or a dish similar to this one. I think my brothers and sisters got a little tired of having it so much, but I never did. After all these years, just the thought of it makes my mouth water. Hope you enjoy it as much as I do! —Linda

1 cup minced onions

1 cup diced celery

1 cup diced red bell pepper

2 cups vegan sausage

1/2 teaspoon sweet basil leaves

1 teaspoon minced fresh garlic

1 1/2 teaspoons sea salt

6 cups canned diced tomatoes

8 cups cooked ridged mostaccioli pasta

Yield: 14 cups

(1/2 cup) Calories 109   Total Fat 2.2g   Saturated Fat 0.2g   Sodium 215.8mg   Total Carbohydrates 16.3g   Fiber 2.7g   Protein 6.9g

Sicilian Stew

1 tablespoon extra virgin
   olive oil

1 medium onion, diced

2 cloves garlic, minced

1 tablespoon diced
   jalapeño pepper

4 cups peeled and cubed
   eggplant

3 cups chopped
   mushrooms

2 14.5-ounce cans diced
   fire-roasted tomatoes

1 cup diced carrots

1 tablespoon drained and
   rinsed capers

1/2 teaspoon dried savory

1/2 teaspoon ground
   coriander

1 teaspoon Vege-Sal

1/4 cup Bragg Liquid
   Aminos

1/2 cup red or white grape
   juice

1 cup water

Salt to taste

In a large pot, heat olive oil over medium heat. Add onion and sauté until clear. Add eggplant, mushrooms, and garlic and sauté for 10 minutes, or until eggplant is tender. Add the rest of the ingredients and simmer on low for 45 to 60 minutes. Add salt to taste.

This stew is delicious served over thick slices of toasted garlic bread, or steaming bowls of polenta. To be honest, I couldn't decide which way I liked it best, since both taste equally good. Either way you decide to serve it, you will have a delicious meal and your family and friends just might think you are part Italian! —Cinda

Yield: 8 cups

(1/2 cup) Calories 43 Total Fat 0.8g Saturated Fat 0.1g Sodium 472.6mg Total Carbohydrates 7.8g Fiber 1.7g Protein 1.4g

Ukrainian Vegetable Stew

In a large stockpot heat the oil and sauté the onion until clear. Add all the rest of the ingredients except the Silk Creamer, flour, and fresh dill, and simmer on low until vegetables are tender. Stir the white flour into the creamer, mixing well. Add to the soup and stir constantly until thickened. Add the fresh dill and mix well.

My sisters and I have traveled to Russia several times, and I always enjoyed the delicious soups served at the various homes we visited there. While each family had their own unique blend of seasonings, the basic ingredients always included cabbage, potatoes, and dill. My friend, Martha Pleshka, made this soup for me one night and it reminded me of those wonderful soups I had in Russia. —Cinda

1 tablespoon canola oil

1 medium onion, diced

2 cloves fresh garlic, minced

2 cups diced carrots

4 cups peeled and diced white potatoes

1 1/2 cup diced zucchini

1 cup diced celery

6 cups shredded cabbage

2 cups cut green beans

6 cups water

3 tablespoons Vegeta vegetable seasoning

Salt to taste

2 cups original flavor Silk Creamer

1/2 cup white flour

1 to 2 tablespoons fresh dill

Yield: 16 cups

(1/2 cup) Calories 45 Total Fat 1.5g Saturated Fat 0.1g Sodium 23.5mg Total Carbohydrates 6.9g Fiber 1.2g Protein 0.7g

Mediterranean Stew

1 tablespoon olive oil

1 medium onion, diced

2 cup uncooked lentils

8 cups water

2 teaspoons sea salt
(or to taste)

1/2 cup uncooked barley

2 vegetable bouillon cubes

1 cup cubed raw butternut
squash

1 cup diced potatoes

1 teaspoon celery salt

1 quart no salt added
whole tomatoes with
juice

1/2 cup raisins

Heat oil in large stockpot. Sauté onion until clear. Add all other ingredients and bring to a boil. Adjust heat to maintain a slow simmer for approximately 1 hour until all vegetables are tender.

The smell alone will almost convince your guests that they are sitting by the seaside at a quaint Mediterranean restaurant! This hearty stew is best served steaming hot with some warm pita bread! Garnish with garlic bread crumbs or scallions. —Brenda

Yield: 12 cups

(1/2 cup) Calories 103 Total Fat 1g Saturated Fat 0.1g Sodium 254.8mg Total Carbohydrates 19.3g Fiber 6.6g Protein 5.7g

Irish Stew With Dumplings

Soak Soy Curls in 2 cups hot water for 15 minutes and then drain. Meanwhile prepare other ingredients. Heat oil in large stockpot over medium heat. Sauté diced onion until clear. Add all other ingredients, including Soy Curls, to stockpot and simmer on low for 1 hour.

For dumplings: In mixing bowl combine flour, baking powder, and salt. Add margarine into flour mixture and cut in with knife or pastry cutter. When margarine is cut into pea-sized pieces, add soy milk. Mix together gently with rubber spatula until dough sticks together. Dough should be slightly moist but not sticky. Drop by teaspoon on top of the cooked stew. Don't dunk under the stew. Cover with lid and cook for another 15 to 20 minutes until dumplings are done. Serve hot!

This stew would also be terrific made in a Crock-Pot, cooking 7 to 8 hours. Just add the dumplings for the last hour of cooking. You can also bake the dumplings in the oven instead of with the stew and serve them on the side. Any way you cook it, it's delicious! —Brenda

1 cup Soy Curls, or gluten of choice

2 cups + 3 cups water

1 tablespoon canola oil

1 medium onion, diced

5 cups chopped cabbage

1 cup diced celery

3 cups no salt added petite diced tomatoes

1 tablespoon McKay's Beef Seasoning (Vegan Special)

1 tablespoon vegetable bouillon

2 cups Imagine Organic No-Chicken Broth, or vegetarian chicken broth of your choice

1 1/2 cups no salt added great northern beans

1 tablespoon dried or chopped fresh parsley

1/4 cup quick or whole barley

1 tablespoon Bragg Liquid Aminos

Dumplings (recipe below)

DUMPLINGS

3/4 cup all-purpose flour

1 teaspoon aluminum free baking powder

1/2 teaspoon sea salt

1 1/2 tablespoons soy margarine

2/3 cup soy milk

Yield: 13 cups stew and 10 1 1/2-inch dumplings

(1/20 recipe) Calories 83 Total Fat 2.2g Saturated Fat 0.4g Sodium 286.7mg Total Carbohydrates 13.1g Fiber 2.9g Protein 3.1g

Latino Black Bean Stew

4 cups water

1 cup diced onion

1 cup finely diced celery

1 cup finely diced red bell pepper

1 clove garlic, minced

1 teaspoon McKay's Chicken Seasoning (Vegan Special)

1 teaspoon McKay's Beef Seasoning (Vegan Special)

1/2 teaspoon low sodium salt

3 cups peeled and diced butternut squash

2 cups rinsed and drained no salt added canned black beans

1 1/2 cups mild salsa

In a medium-sized kettle put the water, onion, celery, bell pepper, fresh garlic, and seasonings and cook on medium-high heat until almost done. Add the butternut squash and salsa and cook 20 to 25 minutes more until the squash is done. Add the black beans and heat to serving temperature. Serve with your favorite corn bread or muffins and a green salad.

Butternut squash is one of my favorite vegetables. I think it really adds a lot of flavor to this stew. Our family really appreciates all the wonderful vegetables God has given us, both for our enjoyment and to help us in our efforts to be healthy. When we girls were growing up, our family had to depend on garden fresh vegetables, as we could not afford the store bought ones. Now that I am older and "wiser," I realize that we were not really poor but very, very rich. God's gifts to us are priceless. —Linda

Yield: 6 cups

(1/2 cup) Calories 76 Total Fat 0.3g Saturated Fat 0.1g Sodium 231.3mg Total Carbohydrates 15.6g Fiber 3.8g Protein 3.2g

Hungarian Goulash

Heat oil in large stockpot over medium heat. Add onion and sauté until clear. Add burger, cumin, chili powder, paprika, and garlic. Sauté another five minutes. Add all other ingredients except for macaroni. Simmer on low for one hour. Add macaroni. Serve hot.

In keeping with our Hungarian heritage, this dish was served often in my childhood home. Mom's version is a little different than mine but equally as good. When finances were particularly tight, this dish consisted of just onion, tomatoes, and macaroni—which was my sister Linda's favorite! In fact, it is still one of her favorites today! Add some fresh whole grain bread and a salad and that's all you need for an awesome meal! —Brenda

1 tablespoon canola oil

1 medium onion, diced

2 cups vegetarian burger

3 tablespoons chili powder

1/2 teaspoon cumin

1 tablespoon paprika

2 cloves garlic, minced

6 cups no salt added
    canned tomatoes

1 cup water

1 teaspoon sea salt

2 teaspoons sugar

1 tablespoon honey

1 1/2 cups cooked great
    northern beans

1 1/2 cups cooked dark red
    kidney beans

4 cups cooked elbow
    macaroni

Yield: 12 cups

(1/2 cup) Calories 104 Total Fat 1.2g Saturated Fat 0.1g Sodium 182.5mg Total Carbohydrates 18.3g Fiber 4.1g Protein 6.5g

Mandarin Beef Stew

2 cups Soy Curls, or gluten of your choice

2 cups boiling water (measure approximate) + 3 cups + 2 tablespoons cold water

2 teaspoons McKay's Beef Seasoning (Vegan Special)

1 tablespoon oil

1 medium onion, diced

2 cloves garlic, diced

1 cup slivered red bell pepper

3 cups sliced baby portabello mushrooms

2 cups diagonally halved snow peas

1/3 cup Bragg Liquid Aminos or Tamari Sauce

1 cup sliced water chestnuts

1 cup whole cashews

3 tablespoons apricot nectar

2 tablespoons honey

2 tablespoons cornstarch

Put Soy Curls into a medium bowl. Add just enough boiling water to completely cover the curls. Add 2 teaspoons McKay's Beef Seasoning (Vegan Special). Let set for 15 minutes then drain and set aside. Meanwhile, prepare other ingredients. Then heat oil in a large soup pot. Sauté onion in oil until clear. Add garlic, mushrooms, bell pepper, and snow peas. When vegetables are "crunchy tender," add remaining ingredients, including Soy Curls, except for cornstarch and 2 tablespoons cold water. Bring to a boil, and then adjust heat to maintain a slow simmer for approximately 1 hour. Mix together cornstarch and cold water and add to stew, stirring well. Continue cooking another 5 minutes until slightly thickened.

This stew is delicious served over brown rice or rice noodles. I like it slightly thickened but it is also good as a soup; just omit the thickening step. I love the flavor of the Tamari soy sauce but Braggs will work too. Soy Curls are wonderful because their texture closely resembles beef. They don't have a flavor of their own, but take on whatever flavor you add. I highly recommend Soy Curls for any recipe that calls for gluten! —Brenda

Yield: 8 cups

(1/2 cup) Calories 125 Total Fat 5.7g Saturated Fat 0.9g Sodium 379.7mg Total Carbohydrates 15.3g Fiber 2.7g Protein 5.6g

Bangkok Stew

In a large stockpot sauté the onion in the olive oil until soft. Stir constantly to avoid burning. Add all the vegetables except the fresh spinach, and sauté until they begin to soften. Add the vegetable broth, coconut milk, curry paste, and seasonings and bring to a boil. Reduce heat to low and let simmer for 30 minutes. Add the fresh spinach and stir until well mixed. Serve over hot brown rice.

Our daughter Catie spent about 9 months as a student missionary at the Bamboo School in Bong Ti, Thailand. While she was there, she learned how to cook some amazing Thai food. When I visited her, we took a cooking class together. It was so much fun learning new techniques and unique flavor combinations. —Cinda

1 cup chopped green onions

4 cloves garlic, minced

2 tablespoons extra virgin olive oil

2 cups chopped mushrooms

2 cups diced carrot

1 cup small cauliflower florets

2 cups small broccoli florets

1 red pepper, diced

2 cups snap peas

6 cups vegetable broth

2 13.5-ounce cans coconut milk

5 tablespoons green curry paste

2 teaspoons Vege-Sal

Salt to taste

2 cups chopped fresh spinach

6 to 10 cups cooked brown rice

Yield: 12 cups

(1/2 cup) Calories 100   Total Fat 8.9g   Saturated Fat 6.6g   Sodium 509.3mg   Total Carbohydrates 4.9g   Fiber 1.1g   Protein 2.1g

Congo Stew

1 tablespoon extra virgin olive oil

1 large onion, diced

1 cup diced celery

1 tablespoon Italian seasoning

1 teaspoon cumin

2 teaspoons Vege-Sal, or vegetable seasoning of your choice

3 large sweet potatoes, peeled and cubed

3 large carrots, peeled and diced

2 1/2 cups cut green beans

3 cloves garlic, minced

1 16-ounce can no salt added garbanzo beans

1 28-ounce can Italian-style diced tomatoes

4 cups vegetable broth

Heat oil in a large stockpot and then sauté onion and celery until onion is clear. Add the seasonings and continue to cook for 1 minute stirring constantly. Add the rest of the ingredients and stir to mix well. Bring to a boil, and then adjust heat to maintain a slow simmer for approximately 30 minutes until vegetables are tender. Stir occasionally during cooking to avoid burning.

I love sweet potatoes! They are some of the most nutritious vegetables around, and are low in fat and calories. An antioxidant-rich, anti-inflammatory food with more than 80 nutrients. Sweet potatoes are native to Central America and are one of the oldest known vegetables. Their sweet and starchy taste give this hearty and satisfying stew a wonderful flavor. —Cinda

Yield: 14 cups

(1/2 cup) Calories 51 Total Fat 1g Saturated Fat 0.1g Sodium 152.9mg Total Carbohydrates 9.4g Fiber 2.2g Protein 1.7g

African Peanut Stew

Heat oil in a large stockpot over medium heat. Sauté onion and celery until onion is clear. Stir frequently to avoid burning. Stir in ginger and garlic and continue sautéing for about 3 minutes. Add the rest of the ingredients except the peanut butter and warm water. Simmer on low for 15 to 20 minutes, until vegetables are tender. Whisk together peanut butter and 1/2 cup of warm water in a small bowl. Add to the stew and cook another 5 minutes until it is slightly thickened, stirring constantly.

If you love peanut butter, you are going to love this thick and hearty stew! It can also be served with brown rice. Don't let the unique list of ingredients scare you; the flavors blend together to create an amazingly delicious and satisfying meal that will make you feel like you are on an African Safari!
—Cinda

2 tablespoons extra virgin olive oil

1 medium onion, diced

1 cup diced celery

1 tablespoon grated fresh ginger

2 teaspoons minced fresh garlic

1 large sweet potato, peeled and cut into 1-inch chunks

4 cups 1-inch chunks peeled butternut squash

4 cups cauliflower florets

1 14.5-ounce can diced tomatoes with chiles

1/2 cup warm water

1/8 teaspoon cayenne pepper

Salt to taste

3/4 cup creamy peanut butter

1/2 cup warm water

Yield: 9 cups

(1/2 cup) Calories 180 Total Fat 12.3g Saturated Fat 2.6g Sodium 100.9mg Total Carbohydrates 13.8g Fiber 3.4g Protein 6.6g

Chili

Minestrone Chili
p. 68

Cashew Chili
p. 61

Wasatch
Mountain Chili
p. 67

Mexican
Corn Chili
p. 57

Five Alarm Chili
p. 55

Chippewa
Indian Chili
p. 60

D1533734

Firecracker Chili

1 tablespoon olive oil

1 tablespoon minced jalapeño pepper

1 teaspoon minced fresh garlic

1 cup low fat vegan chicken, cut into strips

1 1/2 cups sliced green onions

6 cups water

1/2 cup red bell pepper

1/2 cup yellow bell pepper

1/2 cup orange bell pepper

3 cups drained and rinsed no salt added canned red beans

1 teaspoon low sodium salt

1 teaspoon crushed red pepper flakes

1 teaspoon onion powder

1 teaspoon all-purpose veggie salt

2 teaspoons McKay's Chicken Seasoning (Vegan Special)

2 cups cooked rainbow rotini pasta

1 cup Tofutti Sour Supreme

2 cups instant mashed potatoes

In a large kettle heat oil over medium heat. Sauté the jalapeño pepper, minced garlic, and vegan chicken strips until the garlic is a light golden color, approximately 5 minutes. Add the remaining ingredients except the pasta, sour cream, and instant potatoes. Cook approximately 20 minutes until peppers are tender. Stirring constantly with a wire whip, add the instant mashed potatoes to slightly thicken chili. Remove from heat. Stir in the sour cream and add the pasta.

This creamy chili is quick and easy to make and delicious served with whole-wheat dinner rolls, jam, and a colorful salad. I like to make up a couple of different kinds of chili and have a chili night. It is fun to decorate the table in a festive Mexican theme. I love making my family feel that they are as special as our guests! So make up some chili and enjoy the blessings of family! —Linda

Yield: 12 cups

(1/2 cup) Calories 101   Total Fat 2.5g   Saturated Fat 0.8g   Sodium 225.5mg   Total Carbohydrates 16.1g   Fiber 2.8g   Protein 4.1g

Five Alarm Chili

In a large cooking pot heat oil over medium heat. Sauté onion in oil until onion is clear. Add garlic, cumin, and chili powder. Stir for 1 to 2 minutes to allow spices to become fragrant. Add celery and burger. Cook for 3 to 5 minutes. Crush tomatoes and add with all remaining ingredients. Bring to a boil, and then turn heat down to simmer. Cook approximately 1 hour.

This chili is definitely not for the faint of heart! I have many friends who love food that is hot and spicy and it seems I can never get it hot enough for them. Well, hot and spicy lovers, you are in for a real treat. I actually restrained myself with the amount of peppers, so if you like yours extra hot, feel free to be liberal with the portions. If you feel really adventurous, add a teaspoon of the red pepper flakes. (Cayenne pepper and red pepper flakes can be used interchangeably.) Now we're talking chili! —Brenda

1 tablespoon canola oil

1 medium onion, diced

2 cloves garlic, minced

1 tablespoon chili powder

1 teaspoon cumin

1/2 cup diced celery

2 1/2 cups Yves Meatless Ground Round Original or vegetarian burger of your choice

1 cup water

4 cups no salt added canned whole tomatoes

2 cups canned hot (spicy) chili beans (do not drain)

1 1/2 cups drained no salt added canned dark red kidney beans

1/2 cup canned diced green chiles

1/2 cup canned diced jalapeño peppers

1 teaspoon honey or sugar

2 bay leaves

Pinch cayenne or crushed red pepper flakes

Salt to taste

Yield: 8 cups

(1/2 cup) Calories 104 Total Fat 1.6g Saturated Fat 0.1g Sodium 334.2mg Total Carbohydrates 15.1g Fiber 5.9g Protein 8.7g

Mexican Chili

- 1 tablespoon extra virgin olive oil
- 1 large onion, diced
- 1 12-ounce package Yves Meatless Ground Round Original or vegetarian burger of your choice
- 1 16-ounce package frozen corn
- 1 28-ounce can no salt added petite diced tomatoes
- 2 16-ounce cans no salt added pinto beans, drained but not rinsed
- 1 16-ounce can no salt added black beans, drained but not rinsed
- 1 package taco seasoning mix
- Diced avocados for garnish
- Diced tomatoes for garnish

In a large stockpot heat oil over medium heat and sauté onion until clear. Add the burger and continue sautéing for about 2 minutes, stirring frequently to avoid burning. Add the rest of the ingredients and bring to a boil stirring constantly. Reduce heat to low and let simmer for 10 to 15 minutes. Serve hot with diced avocado and tomatoes on top.

This is a great chili to make when you are serving lots of people. You can serve it just like it is, or on a buffet with a variety of accompanying foods that your family and friends can add to their bowls. I like to offer rice, salsa, black olives, soy sour cream, corn chips, and shredded lettuce. Of course, the list can be as long as your imagination! —Cinda

Yield: 12 cups

(1/2 cup) Calories 103 Total Fat 1.1g Saturated Fat 0.1g Sodium 180.9mg Total Carbohydrates 17.8g Fiber 5g Protein 6.9g

Mexican Corn Chili

Place all ingredients in a large kettle and heat to a slow boil. Turn heat to simmer for 30 to 45 minutes. Remove from heat and serve.

I like to serve this delicious chili with homemade corn bread, pure maple syrup, and fresh veggies. Our friends George and Charlene Whiteaker come to Camp Wakonda to help us on the summer work crew. We love sharing meals together. When I served this chili, George said that it was his favorite! Enjoy!
—Linda

4 cups low sodium tomato juice

4 cups water

4 cups no salt added canned diced tomatoes

4 cups drained and rinsed no salt added canned red beans

2 cups fresh sweet corn, cut from the cob

2 cups fresh sliced green onions

1/2 cup peeled and diced green chiles

1 tablespoon sliced fresh jalapeño pepper

2 teaspoons onion powder

1/2 teaspoon cayenne pepper

1 teaspoon low sodium salt

Yield: 16 cups

(1/2 cup) Calories 50 Total Fat 0.2g Saturated Fat 0g Sodium 64.4mg Total Carbohydrates 10.3g Fiber 3.2g Protein 3g

Tex-Mex Chili

1 tablespoon canola oil

1 medium onion, diced

2 cloves garlic, minced

6 tablespoons taco seasoning mix

1 12-ounce package Yves Meatless Ground Round Original or vegetarian burger of your choice

4 cups no salt added canned finely diced tomatoes

2 cups water

1 1/2 cups drained no salt added canned pinto beans

1 1/2 cups drained no salt added canned black beans

1 1/2 cups hot (spicy) chili beans (do not drain)

1 1/2 cups canned creamed corn

1/2 cup diced green chiles

2 tablespoons diced mild jalapeño peppers

1/2 cup salsa of your choice

1/4 cup mild taco sauce

In a large soup pot heat oil over medium heat. Sauté onion until clear. Add garlic and taco seasoning mix. Stir for 1 to 2 minutes and then add vegetarian burger. Cook for 3 to 5 minutes and then add all remaining ingredients. Bring to a boil, and then turn heat down to maintain a slow simmer. Cook for approximately 1 hour.

This is a mildly spicy chili but you can adjust the "heat" depending on how hot the salsa is and the amount of peppers you add. This is good by itself but I sometimes serve it over brown rice and add some homemade corn bread. All you need is a cowboy hat and you will feel like you are a cowhand down on the range! —Brenda

Yield: 14 cups

(1/2 cup) Calories 77 Total Fat 0.9g Saturated Fat 0.1g Sodium 197.1mg Total Carbohydrates 12.9g Fiber 3.8g Protein 5.2g

Sweet Potato Chili

In a large soup pot, sauté onion in oil until clear, then add garlic, cumin, and chili powder. Stir for 1 to 2 minutes to allow spices to become fragrant. Add remaining ingredients. Bring to a boil then turn heat down to maintain a slow simmer. Cook for approximately 1 hour until sweet potatoes are tender.

I absolutely love sweet potatoes. So, of course, when I was thinking up different ideas for chili recipes, sweet potatoes came to mind. I think you'll be surprised at how well they blend with the spicy seasonings of the chili powder, cumin, and jalapeño peppers in this dish. Try adding a cup of black beans or turning up the heat a little with an extra tablespoon of jalapeño peppers. If you are really brave, add a teaspoon of crushed red pepper flakes! A little taste of Mexico right in your kitchen. —Brenda

1 tablespoon canola oil

1 medium onion, diced

2 cloves garlic, minced

1 teaspoon cumin

2 tablespoons chili powder

1/2 teaspoon salt

1 teaspoon honey

1 tablespoon diced jalapeño pepper

1 cup water

1 cup diced red bell pepper

3 cups cubed raw sweet potatoes

4 cups no salt added canned whole tomatoes

1 1/2 cups drained no salt added canned dark red kidney beans

1 1/2 cups drained no salt added canned garbanzo beans

1 cup fresh, frozen, or no salt added canned corn

1 cup mild or medium salsa

Yield: 9 cups

(1/2 cup) Calories 106 Total Fat 1.4g Saturated Fat 0.1g Sodium 135.8mg Total Carbohydrates 20.9g Fiber 4.8g Protein 4g

Chippewa Indian Chili

2 tablespoons extra virgin olive oil

1 medium onion, diced

1/2 cup diced celery

2 garlic cloves, minced

8 tablespoons McKay's Chicken Seasoning (Vegan Special)

1 teaspoon dried thyme

1 teaspoon dried marjoram

1 teaspoon dried sage

3 bay leaves

8 cups water

2 16-ounce cans hominy, drained and rinsed

1 cup wild rice

2 large sweet potatoes, peeled and cut into 1-inch pieces

1 cup frozen corn

1 cup frozen petite peas

1 cup diced red bell pepper

1/2 cup chopped fresh parsley

Salt to taste

In a large stockpot heat oil over medium heat. Sauté onion and celery until onion is clear. Add the McKay's Chicken Seasoning (Vegan Special), thyme, marjoram, and sage and sauté another 1 to 2 minutes. Add the remaining ingredients and simmer on low for 40 to 45 minutes, until vegetables are tender.

Hominy and wild rice were popular foods with the Chippewa Indians. They grew the wild rice in small paddy fields in Minnesota and Wisconsin. This chili would be warm and filling on cold winter evenings. —Cinda

Yield: 10 cups

(1/2 cup) Calories 109 Total Fat 1.9g Saturated Fat 0.3g Sodium 745.9mg Total Carbohydrates 20.6g Fiber 2.7g Protein 2.8g

In a large cooking pot heat oil over medium heat. Sauté onion in oil until onion is clear. Add garlic, cumin, and chili powder. Stir 1 to 2 minutes to allow spices to become fragrant, and then add celery and yellow peppers. Cook 3 to 5 minutes, and then add all remaining ingredients. Bring to a boil, and then turn heat down to simmer. Cook for approximately 1 hour.

Cashews are not the typical ingredient you see in chili recipes, but don't turn your nose up until you try it! My dad thought it sounded pretty silly but when he was sampling all my chili recipes, this was his favorite. I like the texture it adds as well as the taste. —Brenda

1 tablespoon canola oil

1 medium onion, diced

1 clove garlic, minced

1 teaspoon cumin

2 teaspoons chili powder

1 cup diced celery

1 cup diced yellow bell pepper

2 cups canned hot (spicy) chili beans (do not drain)

1 1/2 cups drained no salt added canned dark red kidney beans

1 1/2 cups drained no salt added canned navy beans

4 cups no salt added canned whole tomatoes

1 cup whole cashews

1 tablespoon molasses

1 teaspoon dried basil

1/2 teaspoon salt

Yield: 8 cups

(1/2 cup) Calories 154 Total Fat 5.2g Saturated Fat 0.8g Sodium 181.1mg Total Carbohydrates 22g Fiber 7g Protein 6.8g

Black & White Chili

4 cups water

4 cups no salt added canned diced tomatoes

1 cup mild salsa

3 cups rinsed and drained no salt added canned great northern beans

3 cups rinsed and drained no salt added canned black beans

1 cup sliced green onions

1 tablespoon minced fresh jalapeño pepper

2 teaspoons low sodium salt

2 teaspoons onion powder

1 teaspoon chili powder

2 cups 1/8-inch slices small yellow summer squash

1 cup grated carrots

Put all ingredients in a large kettle except for the summer squash and grated carrots. Bring to a slow boil and cook approximately 15 minutes. Add the carrots and squash and cook 10 more minutes. Serve hot with corn bread and a fresh vegetable salad.

This colorful spicy chili is so good! My husband loves chili and would eat it three times a day if I served it. Thankfully God has provided a variety of delicious foods for us to enjoy. Our Lord has told us in 3 John 2 that it is His desire that above all things we prosper in health. Enjoy! —Linda

Yield: 12 cups

(1/2 cup) Calories 44 Total Fat 0.2g Saturated Fat 0g Sodium 148.2mg Total Carbohydrates 8.8g Fiber 2.7g Protein 2.4g

Great Northern Chili

Put all ingredients except the beans into a large stockpot. Bring to a boil, reduce heat, and simmer until potatoes are tender but not mushy. Add the great northern beans and mix well. Continue cooking only until hot and bubbly.

This is a very simple and easy chili to make. My husband likes to sprinkle a few vegetarian bacon bits on top of his. —Cinda

1 large onion, diced

1 cup finely diced celery

1 tablespoon extra virgin olive oil

3 cups diced potatoes

2 cups water

2 tablespoons McKay's Chicken Seasoning (Vegan Special)

1 teaspoon Vege-Sal

3 15.8-ounce cans no salt added great northern beans (do not drain)

Yield: 8 cups

(1/2 cup) Calories 95 Total Fat 1.1g Saturated Fat 0.2g Sodium 303.9mg Total Carbohydrates 16.5g Fiber 4.6g Protein 5.2g

Pinto Bean Chili

1 tablespoon canola oil

1 cup minced onions

1 teaspoon minced fresh
   garlic

4 cups water

1 cup tomato juice

1 cup mild salsa

1 cup no salt added
   canned diced
   tomatoes

3 cups drained and rinsed
   no salt added canned
   pinto beans

1 cup vegetarian burger

1 teaspoon low sodium
   salt

1 teaspoon onion powder

1/4 teaspoon cayenne
   pepper, or to taste

1/2 cup red bell pepper

1/2 cup yellow bell pepper

1/2 cup orange bell pepper

In a medium-sized kettle, heat oil. Sauté the onions, garlic and vegetarian burger approximately 10 minutes until onions are clear. Add remaining ingredients and cook on medium-high heat for about 20 minutes until peppers are tender.

This quick and easy chili is sure to put a smile on your family's face, especially served with corn muffins and salad. I love how the fresh flavors of the chili send their tantalizing smells throughout our home. Our favorite place to eat is home. After a full day at work, there is no meal so delicious to us as a bowl of chili or some homemade soup. —Linda

Yield: 9 cups

(1/2 cup) Calories 76   Total Fat 1.1g   Saturated Fat 0.1g   Sodium 156.1mg   Total Carbohydrates 12.4g   Fiber 3.5g   Protein 4.7g

Hearty Bean Chili

Add all ingredients except summer squash to a large kettle. Cook on medium-high heat approximately 15 minutes, until onions are almost tender. Add the yellow summer squash. Cook for another 10 minutes. Serve hot.

We like this chili best the second time around as it gives time for the flavors to blend. I serve the chili with corn bread and a fresh green salad. It is amazing to me how many different kinds of beans God has made for us to enjoy! Beans are high in fiber and one serving of dried beans a day can reduce cholesterol by up to 10 percent. The fiber is the primary protector. I try to add beans of some kind to my cooking every day not only because they are healthy ... but because we love them! —Linda

4 cups water

1 cup mild salsa

1 cup no salt added canned diced tomatoes

1 cup plain, no salt added tomato sauce

1 cup diced onions

1 1/2 cups drained and rinsed no salt added canned white hominy

3 cups drained and rinsed no salt added canned black beans

1 cup diced zucchini

1 cup drained Worthington Low Fat Vegetable Steaks, or your favorite gluten, (reserve 1/2 cup liquid)

1/2 cup gluten liquid

1 teaspoon low sodium salt

1 teaspoon chili powder

1 teaspoon onion powder

1/4 teaspoon garlic powder

1 teaspoon cumin

1 teaspoon crushed red pepper flakes

1 cup thickly sliced yellow summer squash

Yield: 16 cups

(1/2 cup) Calories 45 Total Fat 0.3g Saturated Fat 0.1g Sodium 108.8mg Total Carbohydrates 7.5g Fiber 2.2g Protein 3.2g

Three Bean Chili

2 tablespoons canola oil

1 medium onion, diced

1 tablespoon chili powder

1 tablespoon granulated garlic

2 teaspoons cumin

1 teaspoon basil

1/2 teaspoon cayenne pepper

1 teaspoon paprika

3 cups vegetarian burger

1/2 teaspoon salt

1 tablespoon sugar

1 tablespoon parsley

1 2/3 cups drained and rinsed no salt added canned navy beans

1 2/3 cups drained and rinsed no salt added canned pinto beans

1 2/3 cups drained and rinsed no salt added canned black beans

1 quart no salt added whole tomatoes*

*Do not use canned crushed tomatoes. They overwhelm the chili.

In a large soup pot, heat oil. Sauté onion until clear. Add garlic, cumin, chili powder, basil, cayenne pepper, and paprika. Stir for 1 to 2 minutes. Crush tomatoes by hand or with a potato masher and add to pot. Add remaining ingredients. Bring to a boil then turn heat down to maintain a slow simmer. Cook for approximately 1 hour.

This chili is very mild according to my taste buds, but you can make it even less spicy by decreasing the cayenne pepper. Of course, my preference would be to kick it up a couple of notches and add 1/2 cup diced jalapeño peppers. Now we're talking chili! But our niece Crystal loves this one just the way it is and declared this to be her favorite chili ever. —Brenda

Yield: 8 cups

(1/2 cup) Calories 148 Total Fat 2.5g Saturated Fat 0.2g Sodium 241.8mg Total Carbohydrates 22.1g Fiber 7.7g Protein 11.2g

Wasatch Mountain Chili

In a large saucepan heat oil over medium heat. Sauté onions until clear. Stir in the rest of the ingredients, cover, and simmer on low for 20 to 30 minutes. Add more water if it gets too thick.

I serve this unusual, but delicious chili with crumbled tortilla chips and vegan sour cream. I love the flavor and texture that the hominy gives. My husband adds a spoonful of spicy salsa to his bowl. —Cinda

1 large onion, diced

1 tablespoon extra virgin olive oil

2 tablespoons chopped fresh parsley

1/2 teaspoon ground cumin

1/2 teaspoon white pepper

3 tablespoons McKay's Chicken Seasoning (Vegan Special)

4 cups water

1 16-ounce can hominy, drained

1 16-ounce can no salt added great northern beans, drained

1 cup diced carrots

1 cup diced celery

1 cup quick barley

Yield: 6 cups

(1/2 cup) Calories 127 Total Fat 1.6g Saturated Fat 0.3g Sodium 461.2mg Total Carbohydrates 24.4g Fiber 5.4g Protein 4.3g

Minestrone Chili

5 cups water

2 cups no salt added tomato sauce

1 cup mild salsa

1 cup minced onions

3 cups drained and rinsed no salt added canned kidney beans

1 cup drained and rinsed no salt added canned garbanzo beans

1 cup frozen small lima beans

1 tablespoon minced fresh jalapeño

1 cup thinly sliced carrots

1 teaspoon low sodium salt

1/2 teaspoon cumin

1 teaspoon McKay's Chicken Seasoning (Vegan Special)

2 cups chopped fresh baby spinach

1 cup cooked pasta shells

Put all ingredients except the spinach and pasta into a large kettle. Cook on medium-high approximately 20 to 25 minutes. Add the spinach and cook for another 3 to 5 minutes and take off the stove. Just before serving add the cooked pasta shells.

I love how the rich flavors of this chili blend together. And it is full of lots of vitamins and antioxidants. I like to make up an extra kettle of this chili and take it and some of my homemade bread to share with my neighbors. It always brings joy to my heart to do something special for someone else. I have found that it is truly more blessed to give than to receive. —Linda

Yield: 8 cups

(1/2 cup) Calories 109   Total Fat 0.7g   Saturated Fat 0.1g   Sodium 167.5mg   Total Carbohydrates 20.4g   Fiber 4.6g   Protein 5.7g

Mediterranean Vegetable Chili

In a large stockpot heat oil over medium heat and sauté onion until almost clear. Add the eggplant and red pepper and continue sautéing until eggplant is slightly browned and tender. Add the zucchini, beans, tomatoes, and seasonings and stir well. In a small bowl stir the 2 cups of water with the 2 tablespoons of tomato paste until well mixed. Pour into the vegetable mixture and stir well. Bring just to a boil, reduce the heat, cover, and simmer gently for 35 to 45 minutes, until vegetables are tender. Serve hot.

My family loves the combination of flavors in this hearty chili. They spoon it over bowls of hot brown rice. Of course, they all add a few shakes of crushed red pepper flakes to theirs! —Cinda

1 tablespoon extra virgin olive oil

1 large onion, diced

1 medium eggplant, peeled and cut into 1 inch cubes

1 large red bell pepper, chopped

2 cups chopped zucchini

1 16-ounce can no salt added dark red kidney beans

1 16-ounce can no salt added cannellini beans

2 14.5-ounce cans no salt added petite diced tomatoes

3 cloves garlic, minced

1 tablespoon chili powder

1/2 teaspoon cumin

1/2 teaspoon dried oregano

2 tablespoons tomato paste

2 cups water

Salt to taste

Yield: 10 cups

(1/2 cup) Calories 105 Total Fat 1g Saturated Fat 0.2g Sodium 21.7mg Total Carbohydrates 18.8g Fiber 5.9g Protein 6.5g

Bulgur Wheat Chili

3 cups + 2 1/2 cups water

3/4 cup bulgur wheat

1/2 teaspoon + 1 teaspoon salt, or to taste

1 medium onion, diced

2 teaspoons olive oil

2 cloves garlic, minced

3 tablespoons chili powder

2 teaspoons cumin

1 cup diced red bell pepper

1 teaspoon fresh or dried parsley

4 cups no salt added canned whole tomatoes

1/2 cup canned pumpkin

1 cup frozen, fresh, or canned corn

1 cup drained and rinsed no salt added canned black beans

1 cup canned hot chili beans (do not drain)

1 tablespoon honey or sugar

In mixing bowl, pour 3 cups boiling water over bulgur wheat and 1/2 teaspoon salt. Cover and cook over medium heat approximately 15 minutes until tender. Set aside. In a large cooking pot heat oil over medium heat. Sauté onion in oil until onion is clear. Add garlic, chili powder, and cumin and stir for 1 to 2 minutes to allow spices to become fragrant. Add remaining ingredients, including the bulgur wheat, and bring to a boil. Turn down heat to maintain a slow simmer. Cook for approximately 1 hour. Serve hot!

My friend Mark Bond inspired this recipe. He is a great cook and told me he had just made a chili with bulgur wheat instead of burger. After sampling his chili, I was amazed that the bulgur wheat tasted so much like the burger! I experimented in my own kitchen and came up with something close to his. I really like the flavor from the pumpkin and the combination of the different beans. I have tried it with navy beans, great northern beans, and lima beans too. Serve this with some homemade corn bread and you're ready for company. By the way, I have a great vegan corn bread recipe in our first cookbook, Cooking With the Micheff Sisters. *—Brenda*

Yield: 8 cups

(1/2 cup) Calories 100   Total Fat 1.3g   Saturated Fat 0.2g   Sodium 262.3mg   Total Carbohydrates 20.5g   Fiber 5.5g   Protein 3.9g

Thai Chili

Blanch squash, cauliflower, and green beans in boiling salted water for 3 to 4 minutes. Drain and rinse under cold water to stop the cooking. Set aside. In a large saucepan over medium heat, heat oil. Add mushrooms, and cook for 4 to 5 minutes until slightly browned. Add the garlic, Thai curry paste, brown sugar, Bragg Liquid Aminos, and 1 can of coconut milk. Stir until well blended. Stir in the remaining can of coconut milk and mix well. Add the cauliflower, squash, green beans, red pepper, and half of the basil. Simmer on low for 15 minutes. Add the rest of the basil and serve hot with hot brown rice.

My daughter Catie tells me that I really need to add a small red Thai pepper to this! Catie learned to love spicy Thai food while serving as a student missionary in Thailand for 9 months. She now eats it hotter than her dad! Thai peppers are very spicy so beware if you are thinking of adding one to your chili. It does add wonderful flavor as well as authenticity to this dish.
—Cinda

2 quarts boiling water

Salt to taste

2 cups peeled and cubed butternut squash

3 cups cauliflower florets

2 cups cut green beans

1 tablespoon canola oil

1 cup sliced mushrooms

4 cloves garlic, minced

2 14-ounce cans coconut milk

4 tablespoons Thai red curry paste

1/4 cup dark brown sugar

3 tablespoons Bragg Liquid Aminos

1 medium red bell pepper, slivered

30 fresh Thai or regular basil leaves

6 to 12 cups cooked brown rice

Yield: 12 cups

(1/2 cup) Calories 89 Total Fat 7.7g Saturated Fat 6.3g Sodium 218.5mg Total Carbohydrates 5g Fiber 1.2g Protein 1.6g

Salads

Blueberry
Almond Salad
p. 93

Pesto Pasta Salad
p. 80

Sweet Corn Salad
p. 89

Guiltless
Potato Salad
p. 83

Thai Noodle
Salad
p. 85

Napa Valley
Chicken Salad
p. 90

Autumn Pasta Salad

6 cups cooked and cooled cavatappi pasta, or corkscrew or twisted pasta of your choice

3 1/2 cups peeled and cubed butternut squash

Salt to taste

4 cups shredded fresh spinach

1 cup chopped fresh arugula

Sage Pesto (recipe below)

SAGE PESTO

1/2 cup chopped fresh parsley

1/2 cup chopped walnuts

1/2 cup fresh sage leaves

2 tablespoons fresh lemon juice

2 tablespoons extra virgin olive oil

1 clove garlic

1/2 cup water

2 tablespoons McKay's Chicken Seasoning (Vegan Special)

Spray a baking sheet generously with the nonstick cooking spray. Arrange the squash in a single layer. Spray squash with the nonstick cooking spray. Sprinkle with salt and bake in a 430 degree oven for 20 to 25 minutes until tender and lightly browned, stirring after 15 minutes. Set aside. Make pesto (recipe below). In a large bowl combine the squash, pasta, spinach, and arugula. Pour the sage pesto over the top and gently toss to mix well. Serve immediately.

For pesto: In a food processor or blender combine parsley, walnuts, sage, lemon juice, olive oil, garlic, water, McKay's Chicken Seasoning (Vegan Special), and salt to taste. Process until well blended.

I love the unusual flavor the sage pesto gives this pasta salad. I sometimes add 1 can of drained and rinsed cannellini beans. When I want to be extra festive, I serve this salad in a hallowed out pumpkin. —Cinda

Yield: 12 cups

(1/4 cup) Calories 45 Total Fat 1.5g Saturated Fat 0.2g Sodium 72.3mg Total Carbohydrates 6.8g Fiber 0.6g Protein 1.4g

Linda's Rainbow Salad

Mix all the ingredients together in a medium-sized bowl. Gently mix in dressing. Garnish with sunflower seeds, tomato wedges, and fresh parsley.

For dressing: Mix all ingredients together in a small bowl. Refrigerate until needed.

For an even more colorful salad, add some small grape tomatoes. This tasty salad is not only colored like a rainbow but is quick and easy to make. I sometimes make it up the night before so the flavors have time to blend. It is also a great dish to take for picnics and church fellowship meals. —Linda

5 cups cooked rainbow rotini pasta, or your favorite rainbow-colored twisted or corkscrew pasta

1/2 cup whole pitted small or medium black olives

1/2 cup julienned carrots

1/2 cup slivered red bell pepper

1/2 cup slivered yellow bell pepper

1/2 cup slivered orange bell pepper

1/4 cup chopped fresh parsley

Dressing (recipe below)

Sunflower seeds, tomato wedges, and fresh parsley for garnish

DRESSING

1/2 cup Grapeseed Oil Vegenaise

1/4 cup Tofutti Sour Supreme

1/2 teaspoon low sodium salt

1/2 teaspoon seasoned salt or to taste

1 teaspoon onion powder

Yield: 8 cups

(1/4 cup) Calories 66 Total Fat 3.1g Saturated Fat 0.6g Sodium 91.2mg Total Carbohydrates 7.9g Fiber 0.6g Protein 1.4g

Tex-Mex Pasta Salad

1 pound rotini pasta, or your favorite twisted or corkscrew pasta

1 tablespoon extra virgin olive oil

2 cups cubed Worthington Meatless Smoked Turkey Vegetable Grain Protein Roll

1/2 cup water

1 cup chopped yellow bell pepper

3 cloves minced garlic

2 tablespoons taco seasoning

1 tablespoon dried parsley

1 teaspoon sea salt

1/2 cup sliced black olives

1 15.5-ounce can no salt added black beans, drained

2 cups halved grape tomatoes

Tortilla chips for garnish

Tex-Mex Dressing (recipe below)

TEX-MEX DRESSING

2 tablespoons fresh lemon or lime juice

1/2 teaspoon ground cumin

1/2 teaspoon sea salt

1/2 cup Toffuti Sour Supreme

1/2 cup Grapeseed Oil Vegenaise

2 to 3 teaspoons diced jalapeño peppers

Cook pasta according to package directions. Drain, rinse with cold water, drain again, and set aside. In a large saucepan, heat oil and sauté cubed meatless turkey until lightly browned. Add the water, yellow pepper, garlic, taco seasoning, parsley, and salt. Continue to sauté for 4 to 5 minutes, stirring frequently to avoid burning. Combine pasta, vegan turkey mixture, olives, beans, and tomatoes in a large bowl and stir well. Pour salad dressing over the salad and toss gently to coat. Serve with crumbled tortilla chips over the top.

For dressing: Mix ingredients together. Refrigerate until needed.

This salad is a meal in itself! It is always a big hit at potlucks and picnics, and keeps well for several days in your refrigerator. I also like to serve it with corn bread crumbled over the top. —Cinda

Yield: 16 cups

(1/4 cup) Calories 64 Total Fat 2.6g Saturated Fat 0.5g Sodium 114.1mg Total Carbohydrates 7.7g Fiber 0.8g Protein 2.3g

Bowtie Pasta Salad

In large mixing bowl combine all salad ingredients. Pour dressing over salad and toss gently to mix well. Refrigerate 2 to 4 hours before serving.

For dressing: Combine all dressing ingredients in blender except oil. Add oil slowly while blending. Add to salad.

This is a great recipe to make ahead. I like my cold food really cold and my hot food really hot, but if it doesn't matter to you, the salad is ready immediately after making it! I love sun dried tomatoes but fresh grape tomatoes sliced in half can substitute for them. This dish keeps its shape and color really well, so it makes a wonderful salad to take on picnics or for a potluck! Best of all, there are no onions or garlic so no bad breath to worry about! That's a bonus, right? —Brenda

4 cups cooked bowtie pasta

1 1/2 cups drained water-packed artichokes

1/2 cup drained sliced black olives

1 cup frozen green peas

1 cup steamed and cooled 1 1/2-inch pieces asparagus

1/2 cup rinsed and drained sundried tomatoes

Dressing (recipe below)

DRESSING

1/4 cup freshly squeezed lemon juice

1/2 teaspoon sea salt

1 teaspoon dehydrated onions

2 tablespoons canola oil

1 teaspoon sugar

Yield: 8 cups

(1/4 cup) Calories 48 Total Fat 1.5g Saturated Fat 0.1g Sodium 66.2mg Total Carbohydrates 7.5g Fiber 1.2g Protein 1.7g

Pesto Pasta Salad

4 cups cooked rotini pasta, or your favorite twisted or corkscrew pasta

1 15.5-ounce can no salt added cannellini beans, drained

1 1/2 cups diced zucchini

1/2 cup sliced black olives

1 cup diced cucumber

2 cups halved grape tomatoes

Pesto (recipe below)

PESTO

3 cups packed fresh basil

1 cup packed fresh parsley

2 garlic cloves

1 tablespoon fresh lemon juice

3/4 teaspoon sea salt

1/2 cup walnuts

1/2 cup extra virgin olive oil

1/2 cup vegan Parmesan cheese

1 tablespoon Grapeseed Oil Vegenaise

Cook pasta according to package directions. Drain and rinse with cold water. Drain again and put in a large bowl with the cannellini beans, zucchini, black olives, cucumbers, and tomatoes. Pour prepared pesto over pasta mixture and stir thoroughly.

For pesto: Put all the pesto ingredients into a blender or food processor. Process until well combined.

I love to serve this salad in hollowed-out tomatoes. Sprinkle the top with chopped parsley and place on a pretty platter. You can also make little appetizers by putting the salad into hollowed-out cherry tomatoes. If you fill the tray with fresh pieces of parsley, the stuffed cherry tomatoes will stand upright and not fall over. Plus, it looks beautiful on the platter. —Cinda

Yield: 10 cups

(1/4 cup) Calories 95 Total Fat 4.3g Saturated Fat 0.5g Sodium 75.7mg Total Carbohydrates 10.8g Fiber 2g Protein 3.9g

Pink Potato Salad

In a large mixing bowl combine all ingredients. Mix well and pour into serving dish. Refrigerate until cold. Garnish with beet slices on top.

Mom was the inspiration for this recipe. She was helping me with food prep when I was creating recipes for this book and I asked her for salad ideas. She remembered tasting something similar to this at a potluck in Saginaw, Michigan, when our dad was a pastor there. I had never heard of pink potato salad and, quite frankly, it didn't sound good. But Mom bragged on it so much that I decided to give it a try. I was blown away! I love just about any potato salad that doesn't have raw onions in it, but this is my new favorite. I wasn't expecting to like it much less love it! Mom can't remember exactly what ingredients were in the original recipe, but she loves this one too. The sweet pickles really make the difference. Bread and butter pickles are good too. Not sure which I liked better, actually. Try garnishing the salad with a flower made with beet slices and a pickle slice for the center. Stunning and delicious!
—Brenda

4 cups sliced, cooked red potatoes

1 1/2 cups rinsed and drained canned diced beets

1 1/2 teaspoons Lawry's Seasoned Salt

1 cup diced sweet pickles

1/3 cup Grapeseed Oil Vegenaise

Yield: 6 cups

(1/4 cup) Calories 52   Total Fat 2.2g   Saturated Fat 0.4g   Sodium 187.2mg   Total Carbohydrates 7.6g   Fiber 0.7g   Protein 0.6g

Three Pepper Potato Salad

6 cups diced and cooked
   potatoes

1/2 cup diced red bell
   pepper

1/2 cup diced orange bell
   pepper

1/2 cup diced yellow bell
   pepper

1/2 cup sliced olives

Dressing (recipe below)

DRESSING

1 cup Vegenaise

1/4 cup cold water

1 teaspoon dill

1 teaspoon onion powder

1 teaspoon low sodium
   salt

In a large bowl combine all the salad ingredients. Mix in the dressing and gently stir together. Place in the refrigerator for a couple of hours for flavors to blend. Serve cold.

For dressing: Whip the Vegenaise, water, dill, onion powder, and salt together and put in the refrigerator until ready to use.

This potato salad is so good that you don't even miss the eggs and mayonnaise made with dairy. The rich colors and tastes of the pepper blend make this salad a delicious side dish for a meal or picnic. I like to serve it with baked beans, sweet corn, homemade veggie burgers, lettuce, and tomato. Yum—now that is a real picnic! —Linda

Yield: 7 1/2 cups

(1/4 cup) Calories 83   Total Fat 5.3g   Saturated Fat 0.9g   Sodium 104.5mg   Total Carbohydrates 7.6g   Fiber 0.8g   Protein 0.7g

Guiltless Potato Salad

Heat oil in a large cooking pot over medium heat. Sauté onion until clear in 1 tablespoon oil. Add celery and continue cooking until celery is tender. Add water and potatoes, celery salt, salt, chives, and McKay's Chicken Seasoning (Vegan Special), and cook until potatoes are tender. Add all other ingredients and simmer for another five minutes. Pour into serving dish. Serve hot, or refrigerate 6 to 8 hours until completely cold.

Finally, a potato salad without all the high fat and calories. This recipe contains no mayonnaise and can be served hot or cold. I love it both ways. I have even added soy milk and made a creamy soup out of it. Talk about a versatile recipe! Try adding dill pickle and olives just to shake it up a bit— after the salad is cold. —Brenda

1 tablespoon canola oil

1 medium onion, diced

1/2 cup diced celery

2 cups water

5 cups diced raw red potatoes (dice in large pieces)

1 teaspoon celery salt

2 teaspoons sea salt

1 tablespoon chives

1 teaspoon McKay's Chicken Seasoning (Vegan Special)

1/2 cup plain flavor soy yogurt

2 teaspoons nutritional yeast flakes

2 tablespoons Tofutti Sour Supreme

Yield: 6 cups

(1/4 cup) Calories 44 Total Fat 1g Saturated Fat 0.1g Sodium 259.2mg Total Carbohydrates 8.1g Fiber 0.9g Protein 1.4g

Chiang Mai Noodle Salad

4 cups cooked oriental noodles or angel hair pasta

2 cups halved sugar snap peas

1 cup slivered red bell pepper

1 cup cubed cucumber

1 cup grated carrots

Dressing (recipe below)

DRESSING

1 cup peanut butter

4 teaspoons dark brown sugar

1 tablespoon white sugar

1 tablespoon dark sesame oil

2 tablespoons lime or lemon juice

2 tablespoons plain soy milk

1 tablespoon freshly grated ginger

1 clove garlic, minced

1/2 teaspoon crushed red pepper or more to taste

1/4 cup Bragg Liquid Aminos

1/4 cup water

In a large mixing bowl, put the noodles, snap peas, red peppers, cucumbers, and grated carrots. Pour dressing over the noodles and vegetables and stir well. Chill until ready to serve.

For dressing: Combine all ingredients in a medium bowl or measuring cup. Mix well. If you like it hot and spicy, add more crushed red pepper.

This is a very simple and delicious salad. You can add grilled tofu and other vegetables for variety. I like to serve this with large pieces of lettuce and let my guests roll the filling in them. —Cinda

Yield: 9 cups

(1/4 cup) Calories 113 Total Fat 7.5g Saturated Fat 1.6g Sodium 113.3mg Total Carbohydrates 8.3g Fiber 1.2g Protein 4.5g

Thai Noodle Salad

Cook pasta *al dente* according to package directions. Drain, rinse with cold water, drain again, and place in a large mixing bowl. Set aside. In blender or food processor, combine: garlic, jalapeño pepper, cilantro, lime juice, Bragg Liquid Aminos, honey, sesame oil, and salt. Process until smooth, stopping occasionally to scrape sides. Pour over pasta. Add carrots, cucumbers, cabbage, and peanuts. Toss well. Garnish with additional whole peanuts. Eat immediately or refrigerate and eat when cold—your choice!

I love hot and spicy Thai foods, but this dish would be considered mild by Thai standards. If you want more heat, I suggest adding 1 to 2 tablespoons crushed red pepper right before tossing the pasta with the dressing and vegetables. Serve this salad the same day that you make it, otherwise the cucumbers will not be crisp. Of course, if that doesn't bother you, go for it! I usually make suggestions of other ingredients you could add or take away for variety, but honestly, I love this combination so much, I wouldn't suggest a change. Make it like it is! You can serve with some brown basmati rice.
—Brenda

1 8-ounce package angel-hair pasta or vermicelli

2 cloves garlic

1 tablespoon canned jalapeño pepper

1/3 cup chopped cilantro

1/4 cup fresh lime juice

1 tablespoon Bragg Liquid Aminos

1 tablespoon honey

1 1/2 teaspoons sesame oil

1/4 teaspoon sea salt

1 cup julienned fresh carrots

1 cup peeled and diced cucumber

1 cup finely shredded cabbage

1 cup roasted, salted, and chopped peanuts

3 tablespoons roasted whole peanuts for garnish

Yield: 8 cups

(1/4 cup) Calories 79 Total Fat 4.3g Saturated Fat 0.6g Sodium 167.6mg Total Carbohydrates 8.7g Fiber 0.9g Protein 3.1g

Pomodoro Bread Salad

8 cups cubed low fat
   Italian bread

2 cloves garlic, minced

3 cups chopped tomatoes

2 cups chopped cucumber

1/2 cup chopped fresh
   basil

1 tablespoon minced fresh
   thyme

1/2 cup extra virgin olive
   oil

Salt to taste

Place the cubed bread on a baking sheet that has been sprayed with a nonstick cooking spray. Spray the top of the bread with the cooking spray and place in a 350-degree oven. Bake for 5 to 10 minutes and remove from oven. Stir and spray again with the nonstick cooking spray. Return to oven and bake another 5 to 10 minutes or until crispy on the outside and still soft in the middle. Put into a bowl and set aside. Combine the rest of the ingredients in another bowl and stir gently until well mixed. Stir in the bread right before serving.

This salad is especially good with garden fresh tomatoes and cucumbers. My husband, Joel, grows the small pickling cucumbers because he knows they are my favorite. They are so crisp and good that I like to eat them with their skins on. You can also serve this salad with the bread in one bowl and the tomato mixture in another one, and let each person mix their own. —Cinda

Yield: 3 cups

(1/4 cup) Calories 116 Total Fat 9.3g Saturated Fat 1.2g Sodium 69.9mg Total Carbohydrates 8.1g Fiber 2.1g Protein 2g

Waldorf Salad Pockets

Place walnuts, grapes, apples, celery, and craisins in large mixing bowl. Pour dressing over salad ingredients and mix well. Refrigerate 1 to 2 hours until cold. Slice pita bread in half. Open pita half and put in 1 piece of lettuce and 1/3 cup salad mixture. Place on platter and serve!

For dressing: Combine all dressing ingredients and blend together or whip with wire whisk until smooth.

This recipe can be made up the day before as long as you don't fill the pita pockets until ready to serve. For variety, try adding pecans, almonds, or cashews instead of the walnuts. I also love to substitute different dried fruits such as currants, cherries, or raisins for the craisins. Try skipping the pita. Just put your lettuce on a plate and place the salad on top. Garnish with flaked, toasted coconut. Yum! —Brenda

1 cup walnuts

1 1/2 cups halved red grapes

1 cup chopped apples

1 cup celery

1/4 cup craisins

Waldorf Dressing (recipe below)

6 pita breads

12 pieces romaine lettuce

WALDORF DRESSING

1/4 cups Grapeseed Oil Vegenaise

2 teaspoons lime juice

1 teaspoon poppy seeds

1 tablespoon Tofutti Sour Supreme

1 tablespoon sugar

Dash salt

Yield: 12 sandwiches

(1/2 pocket) Calories 106 Total Fat 5.4g Saturated Fat 0.7g Sodium 106.8mg Total Carbohydrates 13.4g Fiber 1.8g Protein 2.5g

Cucumber Dill Salad

4 cups thinly sliced cucumbers

1 cup halved grape tomatoes

1/2 cup shredded carrots

Dill Dressing (recipe below)

DILL DRESSING

1/4 cup Grapeseed Oil Vegenaise

1/4 cup Tofutti Sour Supreme

1 teaspoon fresh lemon juice

1/2 teaspoon onion powder

1/2 teaspoon sea salt

1/2 teaspoon seasoned salt

1 teaspoon Vegetarian Express Lemony Dill Zest

1 teaspoon fresh or dried dill

In a medium-sized bowl put the cucumbers, shredded carrots, and small grape tomatoes. Pour the dill dressing on top of the cucumbers, carrots, and tomatoes and gently mix together. Put the salad in the refrigerator for 15 to 30 minutes before serving. Garnish with fresh dill.

For dressing: Mix the Vegenaise, Tofutti Sour Supreme, lemon juice, onion powder, salt, seasoned salt, lemon dill zest seasoning, and dill together. Refrigerate until needed.

I have such pleasant memories of Grandpa Micheff in his garden picking cucumbers, tomatoes, and carrots. He would share the rich bounties with his neighbors and friends. Grandma would turn his hard work into delicious meals—yum! Just thinking about it makes me not only hungry but excited for the day when I will eat that banquet meal in heaven with Grandma and Grandpa Micheff! That is one meal I don't I want to miss. Meet you there!
—Linda

Yield: 5 cups

(1/4 cup) Calories 33   Total Fat 2.5g   Saturated Fat 0.5g   Sodium 129.8mg   Total Carbohydrates 2.4g   Fiber 0.3g   Protein 0.4g

Sweet Corn Salad

In a medium-sized bowl mix ingredients together. Stir in the dressing. Let the salad chill in the refrigerator for 15 to 30 minutes.

For dressing: Mix the Vegenaise, dill, lemon juice, and seasoned salt together. Refrigerate until ready to use.

My husband loves this Sweet Corn Salad. We think it tastes best made the day before and refrigerated until serving time. That way the flavors have a chance to blend together. It is beautiful served on individual plates. Lay a dark green lettuce leaf on a serving plate and put a slice of red tomato on top. Spoon the Sweet Corn Salad on top of the tomato and set by each plate. Garnish with fresh parsley or chives. Enjoy! —Linda

4 cups cooked sweet corn fresh from the cob

1/2 cup diced red bell pepper

1/2 cup diced orange bell pepper

1/2 cup diced celery

1 tablespoon minced fresh chives

1/2 cup sliced black olives

Dressing (recipe below)

DRESSING

1/2 cup Grapeseed Oil Vegenaise

1 teaspoon dried dill

1 teaspoon fresh lemon juice

1 teaspoon seasoned salt

Yield: 6 cups

(1/4 cup) Calories 67   Total Fat 3.8g   Saturated Fat 0.6g   Sodium 116.2mg   Total Carbohydrates 8g   Fiber 1g   Protein 1g

Napa Valley Chicken Salad

2 cups cubed Delight Soy
   Nuggets

1 cup cooked edamame

1 cup diced celery

1 cup chopped walnuts

2 cup halved red seedless
   grapes

3/4 cup Grapeseed Oil
   Vegenaise

Salt to taste

Put all ingredients into a large bowl and stir until well coated and mixed. Refrigerate until ready to serve.

This is a delicious and unique version of an old classic. I like to serve it in a puff pastry bowl on a bed of lettuce when I have a luncheon. It is also great to take on picnics with some pita bread or soft rolls. —Cinda

Yield: 7 cups

(1/4 cup) Calories 95   Total Fat 7.7g   Saturated Fat 1.1g   Sodium 60.9mg   Total Carbohydrates 4.5g   Fiber 0.9g   Protein 2.2g

Crisp Autumn Salad

In a medium-sized bowl mix the apples, celery, and cranberries together. Pour dressing over the apples, celery, and cranberries. Let the apple mixture sit in the refrigerator until ready to serve. Just before serving, add the lettuce and walnuts. Garnish with extra cranberries and walnuts if desired.

For dressing: Put all dressing ingredients into a small bowl. Mix together until smooth and refrigerate until needed.

I love the beauty of autumn with its colorful leaves, crisp apples, and cool weather. My husband and I love to go motor-biking to enjoy the scenery and then come home and enjoy this simple but delicious autumn salad. I make it ahead of time and then add the lettuce and walnuts just before serving. Sometimes I roast the walnuts in the microwave or oven until slightly browned and then toss them in the salad. Enjoy! —Linda

1 cup thinly sliced red apples

1 cup thinly sliced yellow apples

1/2 cup dried cranberries

1/2 cup diced celery

2 cups chopped romaine lettuce

1/2 cup chopped walnuts

DRESSING

1/4 cup Grapeseed Oil Vegenaise

1 tablespoon vanilla-flavored soy milk

1 tablespoon pure maple syrup

Yield: 5 cups salad, 6 tablespoons dressing

(1/4 cup) Calories 57 Total Fat 3.9g Saturated Fat 0.5g Sodium 20.2mg Total Carbohydrates 5.6g Fiber 0.8g Protein 0.6g

Polynesian Salad

4 cups bite-sized pieces romaine lettuce

4 cups fresh baby spinach

1 cup mandarin orange segments

1/2 cup pineapple tidbits

1/2 cup toasted almond slivers

1/2 + 1/2 cup lightly toasted coconut

Pineapple Dressing (recipe below), chilled

PINEAPPLE DRESSING

2 tablespoons lemon juice

1/4 cup pineapple juice

2 tablespoons Tofutti Better Than Cream Cheese

2 teaspoons sugar

Dash salt

1 teaspoon cornstarch

Combine all salad ingredients, except for 1/2 cup of the toasted coconut, in a large bowl. Just before serving pour dressing over all ingredients and toss well. Serve on individual salad plates or in a large, chilled serving bowl. Garnish with remaining coconut.

For dressing: Combine all dressing ingredients in a blender and blend until smooth. Pour into sauce pan and cook until thickened. Cool slightly and then refrigerate. Add dressing to salad and toss just before serving.

I spoke at a church in Kauai, Hawaii, where a similar salad was served at their potluck. I liked it so much I came home and re-created it. —Brenda

Yield: 10 cups

(1/4 cup) Calories 37 Total Fat 2.5g Saturated Fat 1.4g Sodium 8.4mg Total Carbohydrates 3.5g Fiber 0.5g Protein 0.8g

Blueberry Almond Salad

Mix the lettuce together. Divide onto individual plates. Arrange fruit on top of lettuce and sprinkle with nuts. Serve with dressing on the side.

For dressing: Mix all the dressing ingredients together until blended. Refrigerate until needed.

This salad makes up beautifully on individual plates. I also layer the salad and fruit in a large bowl and top with a strawberry rose and almonds. Whichever way you choose to serve this salad, it is delicious and is sure to please! —Linda

4 cups rinsed, drained, torn into bite-sized pieces green leaf lettuce

2 cups rinsed, drained, torn into bite-sized pieces romaine lettuce

1 cup rinsed and halved strawberries

1 cup rinsed and drained blueberries

1 cup drained mandarin oranges

1/2 cup slivered almonds for garnish, optional

Orange Poppy Seed Dressing (recipe below)

ORANGE POPPY SEED DRESSING

1/2 cup Grapeseed Oil Vegenaise

1 teaspoon fresh lemon juice

1 tablespoon orange juice concentrate

1 tablespoon pure maple syrup

1 teaspoon poppy seeds

1/2 teaspoon low sodium salt

Yield: 10 cups salad, 10 tablespoons dressing

(1/4 cup) Calories 36 Total Fat 2.7g Saturated Fat 0.4g Sodium 32.4mg Total Carbohydrates 2.6g Fiber 0.6g Protein 0.5g

Sandwiches

Grilled Queso
Sandwich
p. 100

Chik'n Pita Sandwich
p. 112

Game Day
Sandwich
p. 99

Cornwall
Pasties
p. 115

Greek Garden Wraps
p. 105

Texas Burgers
p. 107

Curried Chicken Salad Sandwich

2 cups small sliced Delight
   Soy Nuggets

1 cup raisins

1/2 cup cashews

1/2 cup diced celery

7 tablespoons Grapeseed
   Oil Vegenaise

2 teaspoons curry powder

Your choice of bread,
   optional

Mix chicken nuggets, raisins, cashews, and celery together in a bowl and set aside. In a small bowl mix the Vegenaise and curry powder together. Pour over the vegan chicken mixture and stir until well mixed.

I made this for my sister Brenda one day for lunch and she absolutely loved it! I love the texture and taste of the Delight Soy vegan chicken. You can order it directly from the manufacturer if your local market does not carry it. You can also use your own favorite vegan chicken. This filling is delicious in a sandwich or it can be served on a bed of lettuce as a salad. —Cinda

Yield: 4 cups

(1/4 cup) Calories 110 Total Fat 7g Saturated Fat 1.2g Sodium 77mg Total Carbohydrates 10.1g Fiber 0.9g Protein 2.11g

Game Day Sandwich

Mix the Vegenaise and seasoned salt together and set aside. Grate or mash the vegan hot dogs. In a medium-sized mixing bowl add the mashed vegan hot dogs, celery, and red bell pepper. Mix in seasoned Vegenaise. Put the sandwich spread in the refrigerator until ready to use.

My husband and I like to eat light meals in the evening. Maybe just fruit or fruit salad and some popcorn. But if we are doing hard physical labor and are really hungry, we add a good wholesome sandwich like this one to our meal. Serve this sandwich spread on your favorite whole wheat bread with a slice of tomato and a fresh lettuce leaf. Enjoy! —Linda

3/4 cup Vegenaise

1/4 teaspoon seasoned salt

10 of your favorite fat free, vegan hot dogs (about 20 ounces)

1/2 cup diced celery

1/2 cup minced red bell pepper

Yield: 3 1/4 cups

(1/4 cup) Calories 116   Total Fat 8.7g   Saturated Fat 1.5g   Sodium 199.84mg   Total Carbohydrates 1.5g   Fiber 0.2g   Protein 5.5g

Grilled Queso Sandwich

2 cups water

2/3 cup nutritional yeast flakes

1/3 cup all-purpose flour

1/4 cup oil

1 4-ounce jar pimentos

2 tablespoons cornstarch

2 tablespoons lemon juice

2 teaspoons sea salt

1 teaspoon onion powder

1/4 teaspoon garlic powder

1/2 cup diced green chiles

1 tablespoon diced jalapeño pepper

4 tablespoons soy margarine or nonstick cooking spray

24 slices whole grain bread

Combine all ingredients in blender except for green chiles, jalapeños, margarine, and bread. Blend until smooth. Pour into medium saucepan. Add green chiles and jalapeños and cook over medium heat until thickened. Remove from heat and let cool. Mixture will thicken as it cools. Refrigerate 1 to 2 hours.

Spread 1/4 cup cooled mixture on slice of bread then place another slice of bread on top. Spread soy margarine on each outside slice or spray with nonstick cooking spray and place on a medium-hot griddle or nonstick frying pan. Grill until golden. Flip to grill the other side. Serve hot!

This recipe was inspired by two of our friends, Mellisa Hoffman and Chrystique Neibauer. I had told them that I didn't like any cheese substitutes I had tried. They encouraged me to try their recipe, so I did. I liked it, but asked if I could tweak it a bit. They gave me their blessing and I started experimenting. I am so excited with the outcome! This goes great as a dip with tostada chips, a sauce for cooked vegetables, or anywhere you would want a cheese dip! This is like no other "fake cheese" recipe I have ever tasted. I love it and I think you will too! —Brenda

Yield: 12 sandwiches

(1/2 sandwich) Calories 190 Total Fat 5.2g Saturated Fat 0.8g Sodium 403.3mg Total Carbohydrates 26.3g Fiber 4.8g Protein 11.2g

Pimiento Olive Sandwich

Mash the tofu with a fork. Stir in pimientos and olives. In a small bowl mix the Vegenaise, Tofutti Sour Supreme, and all the seasonings together. Stir into the tofu mixture. Chill until cold.

This is a fast and nutritious sandwich. Choose your favorite whole wheat bread and add any combination sliced tomatoes, onions, and leafy green lettuce. This spread is also good rolled up in a spinach tortilla wrap. We like to eat it on our toast for breakfast. Whatever way you choose to serve this filling, it will be enjoyed by your family and friends! —Linda

1 12.3-ounce box Mori-Nu tofu

2 tablespoons diced pimientos

1/4 cup sliced or chopped olives

1/4 cup Grapeseed Oil Vegenaise

1/4 cup Tofutti Sour Supreme

1/4 teaspoon onion powder

1/4 teaspoon low sodium salt

3/4 teaspoon McKay's Chicken Seasoning (Vegan Special)

1 tablespoon chives

1/8 teaspoon turmeric

Yield: 2 1/4 cups

(1/4 cup) Calories 87 Total Fat 6.4g Saturated Fat 1.3g Sodium 176.1mg Total Carbohydrates 3.7g Fiber 0.2g Protein 3g

Spicy Southwestern Wraps

1 cup cooked fresh sweet corn (approximately 2 ears)

1 tablespoon canola oil

1 cup minced onions

1 tablespoon minced fresh garlic

1/2 teaspoon red pepper flakes

1/2 teaspoon chili powder

1 teaspoon McKay's Chicken Seasoning (Vegan Special)

1/2 teaspoon sea salt

2 cups cooked brown rice

1/4 cup sliced black olives

1 cup rinsed and drained no salt added canned black beans

1 cup mild salsa

8 tablespoons Tofutti Sour Supreme

8 8-inch fat free tortilla wraps, warmed

2 cups shredded romaine lettuce

Cook the corn by the method you prefer. Cut the kernels from the cob and set aside. Heat oil in a large skillet on medium-high heat. Add the garlic, onions, sweet corn, and all the seasonings to the skillet and sauté until tender. Stir in the brown rice, black beans, olives, and salsa. Sauté for another 5 minutes and then take the skillet off the burner.

Slightly warm the tortillas approximately 5 seconds in the microwave. On each tortilla put 1/2 cup of the rice mixture in the middle of the wrap and spread it almost to the bottom of the wrap. Spread 1 tablespoon of Tofutti Sour Supreme on top and put 1/4 cup of chopped lettuce on top of that. Fold bottom of wrap up and over vegetables covering 1/4 of wrap. Next fold one side over and keep rolling in tight roll. Serve immediately.

I like to serve this sandwich with tortilla chips, salsa, and guacamole. We love Mexican food and enjoy this delicious but simple meal with our family and friends. The filling can be made up the night before and reheated in the microwave. Then just fill the warmed wraps and put them on a colorful tray. Put a small bowl of salsa garnished with cilantro in the middle of the tray. Enjoy! —Linda

Yield: 8 wraps

(1/2 wrap) Calories 141 Total Fat 2.8g Saturated Fat 0.7g Sodium 314.1mg Total Carbohydrates 27.8g Fiber 6g Protein 4.34g

Potato Spinach Wraps

Melt margarine in a medium stockpot over medium heat. Sauté onions until onion is clear. Add seasonings and fresh spinach and sauté until tender. Add potatoes and lemon juice. Cook filling for fifteen minutes. Set aside. Heat wraps on both sides in a nonstick skillet. Place 1/2 cup filling in center of each heated wrap. Fold bottom of wrap up and over vegetables covering 1/4 of wrap. Next fold one side over and keep rolling in tight roll. Serve hot.

I love Indian food. The curry and cumin in this dish really come through with a wonderful blended flavor. For a more authentic touch, serve in pita bread that has been heated in a skillet with a little margarine. You will be pleased at how much this resembles the taste of a typical naan. Serve the wraps with saffron rice and dahl, and you'll almost think you are in India. —Brenda

2 tablespoons soy margarine

2 medium onions, diced

1/2 teaspoon sea salt

1 teaspoon cumin

1 teaspoon chili powder

2 tablespoons curry powder

1 tablespoon mustard seeds

8 cups chopped fresh baby spinach

2 to 3 tablespoons freshly squeezed lemon juice

3 cups diced and cooked potatoes

10 whole grain wraps

Yield: 10 wraps

(1/2 wrap) Calories 134 Total Fat 5g Saturated Fat 0.9g Sodium 321.6mg Total Carbohydrates 20.7g Fiber 3.7g Protein 4.2g

Don-Bon Wraps

6 large fat free, whole wheat flour tortillas

24 slices Tofurkey or your favorite vegan turkey slices

1 14-ounce can whole berry cranberry sauce

Homemade Stuffing (recipe below)

HOMEMADE STUFFING

2 tablespoons soy margarine

1/2 small onion, chopped

1/2 cup chopped celery

1/2 cup chopped fresh mushrooms

1 1/2 cup water

1 1/2 tablespoons McKay's Chicken Seasoning (Vegan Special)

3 cups of your favorite stuffing mix

1 1/2 teaspoons dried sage

Yield: 3 1/2 cups

Place 4 vegan turkey slices down the center of the tortillas. Spread with 2 to 3 tablespoons of the cranberry sauce, and then add 1 slice of the homemade stuffing. Fold bottom of wrap up and over vegetables covering 1/4 of wrap. Next fold one side over and keep rolling in tight roll.

For stuffing: Sauté onions in soy margarine until clear. Combine with remaining stuffing ingredients in a large mixing bowl. Stir well. Place in an 8" x 8" baking dish that has been sprayed with nonstick cooking spray. Bake in a 375-degree oven for 30 minutes, or until top is golden brown.

Our good friends Don and Bonnie Laing inspired this sandwich, so I named it in their honor! What a wonderful way to enjoy leftovers during the holidays. However, you don't have to wait for the holidays to enjoy this delicious sandwich. It is good any time of the year. You can pack each ingredient separately in your picnic basket and let people assemble their own sandwich at your picnic site. —Cinda

Yield: 6 wraps

(1/2 wrap) Calories 278 Total Fat 3.5g Saturated Fat 0.7g Sodium 930.9mg Total Carbohydrates 53.5g Fiber 6.9g Protein 11g

Greek Garden Wraps

Spread 1/8 cup hummus on a wrap. Layer spinach, tomatoes, cucumbers, carrots, and avocados in the center of the wrap. Fold bottom of wrap up and over vegetables covering 1/4 of wrap. Next fold one side over and keep rolling in tight roll. Serve on individual plates or platter. Garnish with carrot curls and apple slices.

This sandwich is good as a wrap or in a pita pocket. If there are any ingredients you don't care for, just leave them out or substitute. Some other ingredients that I recommend are diced walnuts, pepperoncini peppers, green olives, sweet red bell peppers, alfalfa sprouts, romaine lettuce, sliced beets, sliced apples, and anything your imagination comes up with. I say, "Go for it!" Onion lovers won't want to miss this opportunity for some sweet Bermuda onion slices—but that is not for me. My love affair with onions doesn't start until they are cooked. —Brenda

For hummus: Place all ingredients in blender and process till smooth. Pour into a container with a lid and refrigerate until cold. Spread on wraps or pita pockets or use as a dip for vegetables, baked pita triangles, or your favorite whole wheat crackers.

Here are two great hummus recipes. One has a more traditional flavor and the other has a little more zip! I love them both but just to confuse you, try adding 1 to 2 tablespoons diced jalapeño peppers to the plain hummus recipe for a jalapeño flavor! Honestly! Now I really can't decide which one is my favorite! —Brenda

1 1/2 cups hummus (recipes below)

12 whole wheat or spinach wraps

6 cups baby spinach

8 medium tomatoes

4 medium cucumbers, sliced

1 1/2 cups shredded carrots

4 avocados

Salt to taste

HUMMUS

2 14-ounce cans no salt added chick peas, drained

4 tablespoons sesame tahini

2 cloves garlic

7 tablespoons lemon juice

1/2 teaspoon sea salt

Yield: 3 cups

RED PEPPER HUMMUS

1 14-ounce can no salt added chick peas, drained

2 tablespoons sesame tahini

1 clove garlic

3 tablespoons lemon juice

1/2 teaspoon sea salt

1/2 cup roasted red peppers

Yield: 2 cups

Yield: 12 wraps

(1/2 wrap) Calories 180   Total Fat 9g   Saturated Fat 1.3g   Sodium 286.8mg   Total Carbohydrates 22.7g   Fiber 6.5g   Protein 5.6g

Veggie Burgers

4 cups Yves Ground
 Round Original or
 vegetarian burger of
 your choice

4 cups Pepperidge
 Farm stuffing mix
 or seasoned bread
 crumbs of your choice

4 cups quick oats

2 cups cooked brown rice

1 cup finely grated carrots

2 1/2 cups chopped
 walnuts

1 cup soy milk

1 teaspoon sea salt

1 teaspoon onion powder

1 teaspoon garlic powder

1 tablespoon McKay's
 Chicken Seasoning
 (Vegan Special)

1 medium onion, diced

1 14-ounce package extra
 firm, water-packed
 tofu, rinsed and
 drained

1/2 cup water

Preheat oven to 375. In large mixing bowl combine burger, bread crumbs, oats, rice, carrots, walnuts, soy milk, and seasonings. Mix well. In a food processor, combine onion, tofu, and water. Process until smooth and add to burger mixture. Mix well. Shape into 3-inch burgers. Place on baking sheet with nonstick cooking spray. Bake in 375-degree oven for 20 minutes. Remove from oven and flip each burger. Return to oven for another 10 to 15 minutes or until golden. Be careful not to overbake. Burgers should be tender inside and crispy outside.

These burgers are terrific with most condiments, lettuce leaves, and tomato slices in a hearty whole wheat hamburger bun. I can remember making vegetarian burgers with my mom when I was a child. Back then, we didn't know how unhealthy cheese and eggs were, so most of our recipes included them. But now that I omit them, I don't miss them at all. I was surprised that I didn't need eggs to hold food together. There are so many healthful foods to use as binders: oats, breadcrumbs, and rice being just three! I'll be honest, these burgers almost taste like "the real thing" if you fry them in a little oil instead of baking them. My husband chooses the fried version and I prefer the baked. Try both and make your own decision. —Brenda

Yield: 24 3-inch burgers

(1/2 burgers) Calories 133   Total Fat 6.6g   Saturated Fat 0.5g   Sodium 179.1mg   Total Carbohydrates 13.9g   Fiber 2.5g   Protein 5.6g

Texas Burgers

Stir together barbecue sauce and molasses and set aside. Sauté onion in 1 teaspoon of olive oil until clear, then transfer to a large mixing bowl and add black beans, 3 tablespoons of the barbecue mixture, and remaining ingredients except the 2 tablespoons olive oil. Stir to mix well. Form into 6 patties. Heat the remaining olive oil in a skillet and fry the burgers until first side is crispy. Turn over and brush each patty with the remaining barbecue sauce mixture. Continue to fry until crispy. Watch carefully so they do not burn. Serve on a bun with desired condiments.

My sister Brenda gave these burgers 5 stars! And my panel of testers loved them too. Serve them with the buns and condiments of your choice. They freeze well, so make a double batch and that way you will have them when you need a quick lunch or supper or decide to go on an impromptu picnic. —Cinda

- 1/4 cup hickory barbecue sauce
- 1 tablespoon molasses
- 1 teaspoon + 2 tablespoons olive oil
- 3 tablespoons minced onions
- 1 15-ounce can no salt added black beans, drained and mashed
- 2 cups cooked brown rice
- 3 tablespoons oat bran
- 2 tablespoons minced canned beets
- 1 tablespoon beet juice
- 1 teaspoon chili powder
- 1/4 teaspoon cumin
- 1 teaspoon sea salt
- 1 tablespoon diced pickled jalapeño peppers
- 1 tablespoon cornstarch

Yield: 6 burgers

(1/2 burger) Calories 108 Total Fat 3.2g Saturated Fat 0.5g Sodium 179.4mg Total Carbohydrates 17.4g Fiber 3.2g Protein 3.3g

Grilled Jalapeño Burgers

2 tablespoons diced jalapeño peppers

2 cloves minced garlic

3 tablespoons diced black olives

1/4 cup finely diced red bell peppers

1 small onion, diced and cooked until tender in your microwave or a skillet

1 cup cooked and drained black beans

1 cup cooked and drained navy beans or white beans of your choice

1 tablespoon McKay's Chicken Seasoning (Vegan Special)

1/2 teaspoon ground sage

1/2 teaspoon red pepper flakes

1 teaspoon cumin

1 teaspoon celery salt

1 teaspoon paprika

1 teaspoon chili powder

1/2 teaspoon dried oregano

1 tablespoon minced fresh parsley or dried flakes

1/4 cup seasoned bread crumbs

1 1/2 cup quick oats

1 tablespoon cornstarch

1/3 to 1/2 cup soy milk, as needed

1/4 cup Grapeseed Oil Vegenaise

Salt to taste

6 whole wheat hamburger buns

Combine all ingredients in large mixing bowl. Mix well and then refrigerate for 30 minutes. Preheat oven to 375 degrees. Form 6 round patties. Place on baking sheet sprayed with nonstick cooking spray. Bake for 30 minutes at 375 degrees. Remove from oven. Spray grill with nonstick cooking spray. Grill patties 5 to 8 minutes until done, turning once. When burgers are almost finished, place buns on grill, flat side down, just until golden brown. Place burgers inside grilled buns and serve with your favorite condiments.

If you love a burger with a little heat in it, this is the one for you! I love the flavor that the jalapeño peppers give and the grilled flavor just tops it off! On rainy days, skip the grill, bake 15 minutes longer and enjoy right from the oven or fry with a little olive oil in a skillet! Either way, these burgers are real crowd pleasers. You can make them ahead of time and freeze, cooked or uncooked. —Brenda

Yield: 6 burgers

(1/2 burger) Calories 133 Total Fat 4.9g Saturated Fat 0.7g Sodium 330.2mg Total Carbohydrates 18.8g Fiber 4.5g Protein 4.2g

Gluten Free Pecan Burgers

Preheat oven to 350 degrees. In your blender or food processor blend the tofu, garlic, onion, and Bragg Liquid Aminos until smooth. If necessary to blend completely, stop the blender, stir ingredients, and blend some more. Put the brown rice flour, pecan meal, cornstarch, and nutritional yeast into a mixing bowl. Mix together. Pour the blender contents into the dry ingredients and mix. Add the mashed black beans and stir until ingredients are mixed together. Spray a large baking pan with nonstick cooking spray. Add canola oil and spread around. Spoon 1/4 cup of burger mixture at a time into a round patty and put in the baking pan. The mixture will be soft but will firm as it bakes. Bake approximately 30 minutes, turning the burgers over after 15 minutes.

My friends Jan and Paris cannot eat anything with gluten in it. They have had difficulty finding a gluten-free vegetarian burger that holds together. This gluten-free burger holds together and even those who can have gluten loved them. Serve with gluten-free bread (for gluten-intolerant diners) or whole wheat bread along with lettuce, tomato, onion, veggie cheese, and other condiments you enjoy. The burgers are good as an entrée served with ketchup and homemade oven fries also. Enjoy! —Linda

1 12.3-ounce box Mori-Nu tofu

1 clove fresh garlic, minced

1 small onion

1/4 cup Bragg Liquid Aminos

1 cup brown rice flour

1 cup pecan meal

1/4 cup cornstarch

1/4 cup nutritional yeast flakes

2 cups drained, mashed black beans

2 tablespoons canola oil

Yield: 16 burgers

(1/2 burger) Calories 92 Total Fat 3.9g Saturated Fat 0.9g Sodium 127.7mg Total Carbohydrates 9.8g Fiber 2.2g Protein 4.5g

Black Bean Burgers

4 cups Yves Ground Round Original or vegetarian burger of your choice

4 cups Pepperidge Farm stuffing mix or seasoned bread crumbs of your choice

4 cups quick oats

2 cups brown rice

1 cup finely grated carrots

1 1/2 cups cooked and drained black beans

1/2 cup diced green chiles

1/2 cup tomato paste

2 1/2 cups chopped walnuts

1 cup soy milk

1 medium onion, diced

1 14-ounce package extra firm, water-packed tofu, rinsed and drained

1/2 cup water

1 tablespoon chili powder

1 teaspoon cumin

1 tablespoon McKay's Beef Seasoning (Vegan Special)

1 tablespoon parsley

2 teaspoons granulated garlic

1 teaspoon onion powder

1/8 teaspoon cayenne pepper

1/2 teaspoon sea salt

Preheat oven to 375 degrees. In large mixing bowl combine burger, breadcrumbs, oats, rice, carrots, black beans, green chiles, tomato paste, nuts, and soy milk. Mix well. In a food processor, combine onion, tofu, water, and all seasonings. Process until smooth and add to burger mixture. Mix well. Spray baking sheet with nonstick cooking spray. Shape burger mix into 3-inch burgers. Bake in 375-degree oven for 20 minutes. Remove from oven and flip each burger. Return to oven for another 10 to 15 minutes until golden. Be careful not to overbake. Burgers should be tender inside and crispy outside.

These burgers have just the right amount of spicy and the beans add extra fiber and protein! My husband prefers them fried in a little oil but I like to spare the calories and bake them! Any extras can be frozen in a freezer-safe container and kept for up to 3 months. —Brenda

Yield: 24 3-inch burgers

(1/2 burger) Calories 163 Total Fat 6.8g Saturated Fat 0.6g Sodium 164.3mg Total Carbohydrates 20g Fiber 3.3g Protein 6.6g

Hungarian Sun Burgers

In a medium saucepan, simmer onions in water over medium-low heat until clear. Set aside. Preheat oven to 375. Place the sunflower seeds, flour, and salt into a blender or food processor and process until well ground. Put in a medium mixing bowl and add the onions, carrots, zucchini, V8 or tomato juice, breadcrumbs, and nutritional yeast flakes. Stir well. Form into patties. Place on a baking sheet that has been sprayed with a nonstick cooking spray, and bake for 20 to 30 minutes. Turn the patties over halfway through baking so that they can brown on both sides. Serve hot, or freeze for later use.

My dear friend, Kim Eckenroth, inspired these patties. She made some similar to these during one of our visits to their house. They reminded me of our visit to Hungary where we saw beautiful fields of big yellow sunflowers everywhere. Sunflower seeds are a highly nutritional food that is power-packed with healthy fats and proteins. They are filled with fiber, minerals, vitamin E, and phyto chemicals that are important to our human health. They are among the best foods you can eat to get cholesterol-lowering phytosterols. —Cinda

1 medium onion, minced

2 tablespoons water

2 cups sunflower seeds

3 tablespoons whole wheat flour

1 teaspoon sea salt

2 cups finely grated carrots

1 cup finely grated zucchini

1 1/2 cups low sodium V8 or tomato juice

3 tablespoons breadcrumbs

1 tablespoon nutritional yeast flakes

Yield: 11 burgers

(1/2 burger) Calories 99 Total Fat 7.1g Saturated Fat 0.8g Sodium 114.6mg Total Carbohydrates 7g Fiber 2.4g Protein 3.4g

Chik'n Pita Sandwich

3 cups shredded Cedar Lake Vege-Chik'n frozen roll, or chicken-style product of your choice

3/4 cup Grapeseed Oil Vegenaise

1/2 teaspoon fresh or dried dill

1/2 teaspoon onion powder

1/4 teaspoon McKay's Chicken Seasoning (Vegan Special)

1/4 cup diced red bell pepper

1/4 cups grated carrots

1/4 cup diced celery

4 pita pockets, halved

2 cups shredded green leaf lettuce

2 cups halved grape tomatoes

1/4 cup black olives for garnish, optional

Take the Chik'n roll out of the freezer and thaw overnight in the refrigerator. In a small bowl mix the Vegenaise, dill, onion powder, and McKay's Chicken Seasoning (Vegan Special). Stir until well blended and cool in refrigerator till ready to use. Grate the Chik'n in a medium-sized bowl and add the celery, carrots, and red pepper. Stir in the seasoned Vegenaise. Mix until well blended. Cut each pocket bread in half and stuff with shredded lettuce and Chik'n filling. Top with tomatoes and, if desired, black olives. Serve with your favorite soup.

I made this sandwich filling for my parents and friends Galen and Mickey, and they loved it. Mickey spends a lot of hours helping my mother with kids club and so she appreciates simple but tasty meals. This sandwich filling is also good on homemade bread with sliced tomatoes and lettuce. Some people even like onions on it! —Linda

Yield: 8 pita sandwiches

(1/2 pita sandwich) Calories 147   Total Fat 9g   Saturated Fat 1.2g   Sodium 328.1mg   Total Carbohydrates 7.9g   Fiber 1g   Protein 8.3g

South Pacific Sandwich

In a small mixing bowl stir together the crunchy peanut butter, Better Than Cream Cheese, honey, cinnamon, and pure maple syrup. Mix well. On each slice of bread, spread two tablespoons of the filling. Top with a pineapple ring and a strawberry.

My husband and mother-in-law gave this quick and easy sandwich the thumbs up! Serve this open face sandwich with a colorful tropical fruit salad and a big bowl of yummy popcorn. (The Yummy Popcorn recipe is in our first cookbook, Cooking With the Micheff Sisters.*) We love to make our evening meal the lightest one of the day and it helps us all to sleep so much better! We have found that we still can enjoy making our light meals special by just adding some little decorative touches to our table. For this meal, set the table with an island theme. Put on your favorite music or some South Pacific music, light the candles, and enjoy being family!* —Linda

1/2 cup crunchy natural peanut butter

1/2 cup Tofutti Better Than Cream Cheese

1/4 cup natural honey

2 tablespoons pure maple syrup

1 teaspoon cinnamon

9 slices whole wheat bread

9 pineapple rings

5 strawberries, halved for garnish

Yield: 9 open-faced sandwiches

(1/2 sandwich) Calories 187 Total Fat 8.8g Saturated Fat 2g Sodium 128.5mg Total Carbohydrates 24g Fiber 2.3g Protein 5.9g

Reuben Sandwich

2 8-ounce cans reduced fat refrigerated crescent rolls, or your own bread dough

1/2 cup Grapeseed Oil Vegenaise

3 tablespoons ketchup

3 tablespoons sweet pickle relish

1 14-ounce can low sodium shredded sauerkraut

12 fat free vegan beef slices

1 1/2-cups shredded vegan Swiss cheese, or 12 slices

Preheat oven to 375 degrees. Spray a 17-inch x 12-inch baking sheet with a nonstick cooking spray. Spread dough over entire baking sheet overlapping on the long sides 1 to 2 inches. Mix together Vegenaise, ketchup, and sweet pickle relish. Spread dressing over the dough. Arrange the vegan beef slices down the middle. Spread the sauerkraut over the vegan beef slices and then sprinkle with the vegan cheese. Cut 1 1/2-inch strips on each side of the filling, and alternately fold the strips over the top of the filling. It will look like braiding or weaving. When finished, spray the top with the nonstick baking spray and bake in preheated oven for 20 to 25 minutes, until golden brown. Remove from oven and let set for 10 minutes. Cut into 12 slices and serve.

I make this every year for our holiday party. Everyone loves it, especially my husband. He says the party wouldn't be the same without it! Of course, you don't have to wait until your holiday party to make it. It can be eaten at room temperature, which makes it a favorite for picnics and brown bag lunches.
—Cinda

Yield: 12 slices

(1/2 slice) Calories 128 Total Fat 7.7g Saturated Fat 1.9g Sodium 369.1mg Total Carbohydrates 10.7g Fiber 0.6g Protein 4.2g

Cornwall Pasties

For dough: Bring water and margarine to a boil in a large pan, and then take the pan off the heat. Stir the flour and salt into the mixture bit by bit with a spatula, until a dough forms. Tip the dough onto a floured surface and, using your hands, shape it into a smooth ball. Dust the top with flour, then cover with plastic wrap and chill in the refrigerator for at least 30 minutes.

For filling: Sauté the onion in the olive oil until clear, and then add the garlic, carrots, potatoes, and mushrooms. In a small bowl dissolve the vegetable bouillon cube in 1/4 cup water, add the tarragon, and then pour into the pot with the vegetables. Continue to cook until vegetables are tender, making sure to stir often so they won't burn. When tender, remove the pan from the heat and set aside.

Preheat oven to 350 degrees and assemble the pasties. Divide the ball of dough into 4 equal pieces. On a floured surface, roll each section into an 11-inch circle. Place 1 cup of filling on the dough and fold over. Roll the edges together and crimp with your fingers. Make 3 small slits in the top. Place the pasties on a baking sheet that has been sprayed with a nonstick cooking spray and bake in a 350-degree oven for 40 minutes. Do not overbake, or dough will be tough and too crisp. Let cool for 10 minutes before eating.

My husband and I and our children, David and Catie, recently traveled to England. We traveled throughout the majority of the beautiful country. Catie and I fell in love with Cornish pasty (pronounced pass) and would have one in every city we visited. It is said that they originated in Cornwall, England, where the miners would take them with them to work every day for their lunch. This recipe is similar except the miners always had meat in theirs. You can add any of your favorite vegetables and/or vegan meat substitutes and make up your own fillings. —Cinda

DOUGH

1 cup margarine

1 1/4 cups hot water

2 cups whole wheat flour

2 cups white flour

1 tablespoon sea salt

FILLING

1 medium onion, minced

2 tablespoons olive oil

3 cloves garlic, minced

1 1/2 cups diced carrots

4 cups peeled and thinly sliced potatoes

2 cups chopped mushrooms

1/4 cup water

1 cube vegetable bouillon

1 teaspoon dried tarragon

Salt to taste

Yield: 4 pasties

(1/4 pasty) Calories 282 Total Fat 13.6g Saturated Fat 4.2g Sodium 563.1mg Total Carbohydrates 35.7g Fiber 3.3g Protein 3.9g

Crock-Pot

Farmers' Stew
p. 120

Turkey Noodle Soup
p. 122

Vegetable Vindaloo
p. 129

Three Bean Bake
p.125

Cuban Black Bean Soup
p. 121

Farmers' Stew

2 cups chopped broccoli

2 cups chopped cauliflower

1/2 cup diced red pepper

1 1/2 cups diced yellow squash

3 cups cut fresh green beans

2 1/2 cups peeled and cubed potatoes

1 eggplant, peeled and cut into 1/2-inch cubes

1 cup chopped carrots

2 cups chopped zucchini

1 medium onion, diced

1 cup peeled and cubed butternut squash

1 16-ounce can no salt added garbanzo beans, drained

3 cups homemade gluten or gluten of your choice, cut into 1-inch chunks

1 6-ounce can tomato paste

4 cups vegetable broth

1 cup gluten broth

1 tablespoon extra virgin olive oil

1/2 cup flour

1 1/2 teaspoon Vege-Sal

3 tablespoons Bragg Liquid Aminos

1 tablespoon minced garlic

Salt to taste

Put all of the cut vegetables, gluten, and garbanzos into a large Crock-Pot. In separate bowl, mix the tomato paste, vegetable broth, gluten broth, olive oil, flour, and seasonings. Pour over vegetables and stir well. Cover and cook on high 4 1/2 to 5 hours until vegetables are tender.

This is a very hardy and nourishing stew! I love the flavor the homemade gluten and the gluten broth give. However, you can use canned gluten. A big thick slice of homemade whole wheat bread is all you need to serve with this!
—Cinda

Yield: 16 cups

(1/2 cup) Calories 71 Total Fat 1.3g Saturated Fat 0.1g Sodium 210.1mg Total Carbohydrates 12.4 Fiber 2.7g Protein 3.6g

Cuban Black Bean Soup

Combine all ingredients in Crock-Pot and let simmer on low for 7 to 8 hours. To shorten cooking time, cook on high until the onions and red peppers are tender and then reduce heat.

This soup is similar to one I tasted at one of my favorite restaurants and is delicious served with fresh whole grain bread. I love a little "zip" in my food so if you do, too, add 1/4 cup diced jalapeño peppers! Oh yeah! Now that's what I call soup! —Brenda

1 medium onion, diced

6 cups cooked and drained black beans

2 cloves garlic, minced

1/2 cup diced celery

2 cups water

1/2 cup diced red bell pepper

1/2 cup diced green chiles

1/2 teaspoon sea salt

1/2 teaspoon cumin

1 vegetable bouillon cube

2 tablespoons lemon juice

1 tablespoon Bragg Liquid Aminos

Yield: 8 1/2 cups

(1/2 cup) Calories 88 Total Fat 0.5g Saturated Fat 0.1g Sodium 136.6mg Total Carbohydrates 16g Fiber 5.6g Protein 5.7g

Turkey Noodle Soup

- 1 medium onion, diced
- 8 cups water
- 1 cup braised gluten
- 1 cup diced carrots
- 1 cup diced celery
- 4 tablespoons chicken bouillon
- 1/4 cup barley
- 1 tablespoon dried parsley
- 1 1/2 cups cooked and drained great northern beans
- 1 cup eggless fine soup noodles

Combine all ingredients except for the pasta into your Crock-Pot and bring to a boil. Turn the heat to a slow simmer. Cook for 7 to 8 hours until all vegetables are tender. Add the pasta and continue cooking only until pasta is tender, not mushy. You can also pre-cook the pasta and add right before serving. Serve hot!

I love my Crock-Pot and use it often. If your mornings are rushed, try combining all your ingredients together the night before. Put them in the refrigerator. In the morning, just put everything in the Crock-Pot and turn it on. When you return after a hard day of work, you'll love the tantalizing aroma coming from your kitchen. And best of all, you'll enjoy not having to cook. Just add some bread or crackers and a salad. Enjoy your meal in minutes! —Brenda

Yield: 12 cups

(1/2 cup) Calories 79   Total Fat 1.3g   Saturated Fat 0.1g   Sodium 342.6mg   Total Carbohydrates 12.6g   Fiber 3g   Protein 4.2g

Tomato Vegetable Soup

Combine all ingredients in Crock-Pot and cook for 7 to 8 hours. Serve hot!

I love this recipe because there is almost no prep work . . . just throw everything in the pot and go to bed! Your soup will be ready in the morning. Or dump everything in before you leave for work and supper is ready when you come home! Add some whole wheat bread and a nice green salad to complete the meal. Now this is what I call fast and easy! And a big bonus, it's fat free! —Brenda

1 medium onion, diced

8 cups no salt added canned tomatoes

4 cups water

4 cups frozen mixed vegetables

1 tablespoon chopped fresh or dried parsley

1 tablespoon McKay's Beef Seasoning (Vegan Special)

1/4 cup whole or quick barley

2 cups chopped cabbage

Yield: 12 cups

(1/2 cup) Calories 77 Total Fat 0g Saturated Fat 0g Sodium 104mg Total Carbohydrates 16.7g Fiber 4.9g Protein 3.6g

Country Chili

1 medium onion, diced

1 tablespoon extra virgin olive oil

1 red pepper, diced

1 12-ounce package Yves Meatless Ground Round Original or your favorite vegetarian burger

2 16-ounce cans vegetarian baked beans

1 15-ounce can no salt added black beans, drained

1 15-ounce can no salt added dark red kidney beans, drained

1 15-ounce can no salt added garbanzo beans, drained

1 14.5-ounce can no salt added petite diced tomatoes

1 1/2 cups frozen corn

1 cup diced celery

2 cloves garlic, minced

2 tablespoons chili powder

1 tablespoon dried parsley

1 tablespoon dried oregano

1 tablespoon dried basil

1 teaspoon sea salt, or to taste

1 teaspoon all-purpose vegetable seasoning

1 teaspoon diced jalapeño

In a medium saucepan, heat the oil. Sauté the onion until clear. Add the red pepper and burger and sauté another 3 minutes. Put the burger mixture in the Crock-Pot and add the rest of the ingredients. Stir, cover, and cook on high for 2 hours.

My family loved the taste of this chili, and I loved how quick and easy it is to make! You can add more jalapeños if you would like it to be a little spicier.
—Cinda

Yield: 10 cups

(1/2 cup) Calories 153   Total Fat 1.8g   Saturated Fat 0.3g   Sodium 351.8mg   Total Carbohydrates 27.2g   Fiber 7.6g   Protein 10.1g

Three Bean Bake

Blend the onion in the blender with 1 cup of water. Put the blended onion in the Crock-Pot with the rest of the ingredients except for the cornstarch and 1/4 cup cold water. Turn the Crock-Pot on high and cook for approximately 8 hours until beans are tender. Mix the cornstarch with 1/4 cup cold water and stir until there are no more lumps. While stirring, add to the hot bean mixture. Stir until mixture thickens slightly. Serve hot or cold.

Working on this cookbook was so much fun because I had the privilege of working with Mom in her kitchen. I love cooking with Mom. She is a lot of fun and a real worker bee. She inspires me to never give up and keep trying. Dad helped by tasting the dishes we prepared and let us know if something was great or needed more seasoning. This Crock-Pot recipe can cook all night on high and be ready to eat the next day. I love these quick and easy but delicious recipes. Enjoy! —Linda

1 medium onion

6 cups + 1 cup + 1/4 cup water

1 cup uncooked pinto beans, sorted and washed

1 cup uncooked red beans, sorted and washed

1 cups uncooked navy beans, sorted and washed

1 cup low sugar ketchup

1 cup diced celery

1 cup diced red bell pepper

1 tablespoon sliced jalapeño pepper

1/2 cup shredded carrot

2 tablespoons Sucanat (granulated cane juice)

1 teaspoon low sodium salt

2 teaspoons McKay's Beef Seasoning (Vegan Special)

1 teaspoon Vegetarian Express Pepper-Like Seasoning

1/4 cup cornstarch

Yield: 11 cups

(1/2 cup) Calories 125 Total Fat 0.4g Saturated Fat 0.1g Sodium 105.2mg Total Carbohydrates 21g Fiber 5.3g Protein 6.1g

Mama Mia's Spaghetti Sauce

1 medium onion, diced

2 cloves garlic, minced

1/2 cup chopped celery

1 medium red or yellow bell pepper, diced

2 cups Yves Ground Round Original or vegetarian burger of your choice

4 cups no salt added canned whole tomatoes

2 cups crushed tomatoes

1 cup water

1 1/2 cups canned sliced mushrooms

1 tablespoon sugar

2 bay leaves

Salt to taste

Combine all ingredients in a Crock-Pot and cook on low for 5 to 8 hours.

This is the easiest spaghetti sauce you will ever make! Just dump it all in the Crock-Pot, go about your business, and come home with supper almost ready! All you need to do is cook the pasta of your choice, and add a salad! Sometimes I cook the pasta the night before. Then, right before serving, I put it in a strainer, pour hot water over it, and it's ready to serve! Trust me, it will taste just the same as if you had just cooked it! I love shortcuts—especially when they make my life easier! —Brenda

Yield: 8 cups

(1/2 cup) Calories 57 Total Fat 0.3g Saturated Fat 0g Sodium 142.8mg Total Carbohydrates 10.3g Fiber 2.7g Protein 4.9g

Crock-Pot Barbecue

Blend the onion in the blender with 1 cup water and put it into the Crock-Pot. Add remaining ingredients, except the rolls, and stir until well blended. Cook on high heat for approximately 7 hours. Serve with the homemade rolls.

This barbecue is wonderful for a church potluck or picnic. I like to make it when I'm feeding a crowd at my house. I serve it with potato salad, a vegetable relish tray, and dessert. My husband loves barbecue so is always happy when there is some left over for the next day. —Linda

1 medium onion, chopped

1 cup + 3 cups water

2 cups dried vegetarian burger

1 1-pound 4-ounce can vegetarian burger

1 12-ounce can tomato paste

2 cups low sugar ketchup

1/4 cup Sucanat (granulated cane juice)

2 teaspoons lemon juice

1 cup finely diced celery

1 cup shredded carrots

1 cup finely diced red bell pepper

1 tablespoon McKay's Beef Seasoning (Vegan Special)

2 teaspoons chili powder

12 homemade rolls

Yield: 12 cups

(1/2 cup) Calories 92 Total Fat 0.6g Saturated Fat 0g Sodium 236.4mg Total Carbohydrates 10.4g Fiber 2.4g Protein 5.3g

Spiced Sweet Potatoes & Squash

4 cups diced sweet potatoes

4 cups diced butternut squash

2 tablespoons Sucanat (granulated cane juice)

1 cup 100% pure white grape peach juice

2 tablespoons soy margarine

1/4 teaspoon low sodium salt

1 teaspoon cinnamon

1 tablespoon vanilla

1/2 cup sweetened soy milk

1/4 cup toasted pecan pieces

Put all the ingredients in the Crock-Pot except for the soy milk and toasted pecan pieces. Cook on high for approximately 3 hours. Take out of Crock-Pot, add the soy milk, and whip together until creamy. Sprinkle toasted pecans on top. Serve with stuffing, mashed potatoes, gravy, fresh broccoli, and a colorful salad.

We love sweet potatoes and sweet potatoes are so good for us! They are an excellent source of vitamin A, vitamin C, and manganese. Sweet potatoes are a good source of copper, dietary fiber, vitamin B$_6$, potassium, and iron. Squash contains some strong antioxidant properties, which help to prevent illnesses such as cataracts, certain types of cancer, and cardiovascular diseases. So cook up some sweet potatoes and squash and your body will thank you! Besides, it is mmm *good!* —Linda

Yield: 6 1/2 cups

(1/2 cup) Calories 105 Total Fat 3.2g Saturated Fat 0.8g Sodium 70.5mg Total Carbohydrates 19g Fiber 2.4g Protein 1.4g

Vegetable Vindaloo

Combine all ingredients in a large Crock-Pot. Mix well. Cover and cook on high for 3 hours until vegetables are tender.

Vindaloo is a spicy stew from the Goa region of India. Adding more or less curry powder and hot sauce will make vindaloo mild or spicy to fit your taste buds. It traditionally is made with some type of meat. You can add a vegetable protein if you like. Vindaloo is good by itself, or served over hot brown basmati rice. I like to sprinkle some chopped peanuts over the top. —Cinda

3 cups peeled and diced potatoes

3 cups cauliflower florets

2 15.5-ounce cans no salt added chickpeas, rinsed and drained

2 large leeks, white and green parts sliced into 2 inch pieces, rinsed very well

1 cup frozen peas

1 cup no salt added tomato sauce

2 tablespoons fresh minced ginger

2 tablespoons curry powder

2 cloves garlic, minced

2 teaspoons cumin

1 teaspoon cinnamon

1 teaspoon hot sauce

3 tablespoons fresh parsley

1 teaspoon sugar

1 1/2 cups water

1 teaspoon sea salt

Yield: 10 cups

(1/2 cup) Calories 96 Total Fat 1g Saturated Fat 0.1g Sodium 116.3mg Total Carbohydrates 18.6g Fiber 3.9g Protein 4.3g

Mumtaz Curry

4 cups water

3 tablespoons McKay's Chicken Seasoning (Vegan Special)

3 medium carrots, diced

3 large potatoes, diced

2 cups 1-inch pieces fresh green beans

1 large onion, diced

1 15-ounce can no salt added garbanzo beans, drained

3 cloves garlic, minced

2 tablespoons quick-cooking tapioca

2 teaspoons curry powder

1 teaspoon coriander

1/4 teaspoon crushed red pepper, or to taste

1 1/2 teaspoons sea salt

1 14.5-ounce can no salt added petite diced tomatoes

5 to 10 cups cooked brown rice

Mix together water and McKay's Chicken Seasoning (Vegan Special) and set aside. Put rest of ingredients, except for brown rice, into a large Crock-Pot. Pour the water and McKay's Chicken Seasoning (Vegan Special) over the top and stir well. Cover and cook on low for 8 to 9 hours, or on high for 4 to 5 hours, until vegetables are tender. Serve over hot cooked brown rice.

My family loves Indian food, and this is an easy recipe. The slow cooking enhances the flavors and you're not slaving over a hot stove all afternoon!
—Cinda

Yield: 10 cups

(1/2 cup) Calories 88 Total Fat 0.5g Saturated Fat 0.1g Sodium 406.2mg Total Carbohydrates 18.5g Fiber 3.4g Protein 2.9g

Creole Gumbo

Put all ingredients except the oil, flour, broth, and rice into the Crock-Pot and mix well. In a small saucepan heat oil and then stir in flour. Stirring constantly, continue cooking until flour is lightly browned and fragrant. Slowly add 4 cups vegetable broth and continue to stir until there are no lumps. Pour over the vegetable mixture in the Crock-Pot, mix well, cover, and cook on high until vegetables are tender, 6 to 7 hours. Serve with brown rice.

My husband and I enjoyed our visit to Louisiana, and particularly liked the unique flavors used in the foods of that region. Louisiana is known for its gumbo, which is a thick stew usually made with meat or seafood, and traditionally served with rice. The primary and necessary ingredient, however, is okra, from which the dish derives its name. Gumbo can be spicy or mild depending on your taste. —Cinda

Yield: 14 cups

1 large onion, diced

1/2 cup diced red pepper

3/4 cup diced celery

1 clove garlic, minced

3 cups sliced okra

2 cups finely diced zucchini

1 cup diced leek

1 sweet potato, peeled and cubed

2 medium carrots, diced

2 cups fresh or frozen corn

1 28-ounce can no salt added petite diced tomatoes

1 teaspoon Vege-Sal

1/2 cup white grape juice

1/2 cup water

1/4 teaspoon Tabasco sauce, or your favorite hot sauce

1/4 teaspoon paprika

2 tablespoons chopped fresh parsley

1 tablespoon dried or fresh basil

1/2 teaspoon allspice

1 teaspoon dried thyme

3 bay leaves

1/4 cup canola oil

1/2 cup flour

4 cups vegetable broth

8 cups cooked brown rice

(1/2 cup) Calories 65 Total Fat 2.5g Saturated Fat 0.2g Sodium 95.5mg Total Carbohydrates 10.1g Fiber 1.9g Protein 1.6g

Emperor's Chow Mein

4 cups + 2 tablespoons water

1 medium onion, diced

1/2 cup Imagine Organic No-Chicken Broth

1 cup diced cabbage

1/2 cup slivered celery

1/2 cup sliced carrots

1 cup sliced water chestnuts

1 1/2 cups fresh bean sprouts

1/2 teaspoon powdered mustard

1 large vegetable bouillon cube

1 tablespoon McKay's Chicken Seasoning (Vegan Special)

3 tablespoons Bragg Liquid Aminos

Pinch crushed red pepper flakes

1 cup gluten of your choice

2 tablespoons corn starch

4 to 8 cups cooked brown rice

Diced scallions for garnish

Combine all ingredients except the 2 teaspoons water, cornstarch, rice, and scallions in a Crock-Pot and cook on low for 5 to 8 hours. Combine 2 teaspoons water and 2 teaspoons cornstarch and mix until smooth. Add to Crock-Pot, turn heat to high and continue cooking for 30 minutes or until thickened. Serve hot over hot brown rice and garnish with fresh scallions.

Slow cookers like Crock-Pots really can make your life easier and your recipe options are endless, although most people think of them for only soup or beans. This recipe is so simple and tastes good too. You can even make it up several days ahead of time, although I don't recommend freezing it. —Brenda

Yield: 4 cups

(1/2 cup) Calories 53 Total Fat 0.6g Saturated Fat 0g Sodium 638.8mg Total Carbohydrates 9.5g Fiber 1.6g Protein 4.8g

Cabbage Rolls

Bring water in a large kettle to a boil. Meanwhile, cut the core out of the middle of the cabbage. Carefully put the head of cabbage into the boiling water. With a pair of tongs gently pull the leaves off of the cabbage and place them on a large plate. When all the leaves are off, remove the kettle from the stove and pour out the water.

In a medium skillet heat oil over medium heat and then sauté the diced onion, garlic, and burger. When the onion is cooked, add the raw rice, salt, onion powder, and McKay's Beef Seasoning (Vegan Special). Remove the mixture from the burner.

Take a cabbage leaf and carefully shave the vein of the leaf with a knife so it will not be so thick when it is rolled. Put 1/4 cup of rice mixture in each leaf and roll, making sure the ends are tucked in tightly.

Line the Crock-Pot with several cabbage leaves. Place the cabbage rolls on top of the leaves. Pour sauerkraut and diced tomatoes on top of all the cabbage rolls. Put any leftover cabbage leaves on top. Pour 3 cups water over the cabbage and put the lid on. Turn the Crock-Pot on high and cook approximately 7 hours until rice is at the desired tenderness.

You can also cook this dish on high in your rice cooker for approximately 2 1/2 hours until rice is tender.

1 medium-sized head cabbage

1/2 cup diced onions

1/4 teaspoon minced garlic

1 tablespoon canola oil

1 cup vegetarian burger

1 3/4 cups brown basmati rice

2 teaspoons low sodium salt

1 teaspoon onion powder

1 teaspoon McKay's Beef Seasoning (Vegan Special)

4 cups no salt added canned tomatoes

1/2 cup low sodium sauerkraut

3 cups water

This is a spin off of our family's traditional Hungarian dish. I think the brown rice and minced garlic enhance the flavor. When I was a little girl, every time our mom would say we were going to Grandma's, my mouth would start watering just thinking of her delicious cabbage rolls. They are so good!
—Linda

Yield: 12 cabbage rolls

(1 cabbage roll) Calories 81 Total Fat 1.6g Saturated Fat 0.1g Sodium 353.9mg Total Carbohydrates 13.6g Fiber 2.8g Protein 4.1g

Cinnamon Applesauce

16 cups peeled and diced apples

3 cups pure white grape peach juice

1 teaspoon cinnamon

Wash, peel, and dice apples. Put apples in Crock-Pot. Add pure white grape peach juice and cinnamon. Set Crock-Pot on high and cook for 7 to 8 hours. Mash apples with a hand masher to desired consistency.

This applesauce can also be made in a rice cooker: Put apples, cinnamon, and 5 to 6 cups grape peach juice in a rice cooker. Cook for about 2 hours. Open rice cooker carefully to avoid steam burns. Take a hand masher and mash the apples and juice. Shut the lid and cook minutes 30 minutes longer until apples are completely soft. Cool and enjoy!

This no-fuss applesauce is so good. Instead of the grape peach juice, you can use apple juice or another favorite juice. For pink applesauce, try raspberry cranberry juice. I like this applesauce because I can start it first thing in the morning in the rice cooker or in the Crock-Pot just before going to bed. I like to use two or three different kinds of apples for a richer flavor. My family loves it when I make toast with peanut butter and top it with hot applesauce—a meal that is so simple to make but oh so good and nutritious! —Linda

Yield: 9 cups

(1 cup) Calories 144 Total Fat 0g Saturated Fat 0g Sodium 5.1mg Total Carbohydrates 38.2g Fiber 2.7g Protein 0.5g

Brown Rice Breakfast Cereal

Put water, rice, and salt in the Crock-Pot. Cook on high for 2 1/2 hours. (If you made more than enough rice, remove the extra and reserve for another meal.) Add soy milk creamer or soy milk, maple syrup, vanilla, and dash of cinnamon. Serve with fresh fruit and nuts and enjoy!

This cereal can be put in the Crock-Pot early in the morning so that it is ready by breakfast time. Sometimes before I add the soy milk, pure maple syrup, and seasonings, I take out half the rice to use for patties or a casserole. Then I add the soy milk and the rest of the ingredients to make the cereal. If you decide to do that, just cut down on the milk used to make the creamy rice cereal. So cook up some rice and enjoy all the wonderful dishes you can create with this simple but nutritious food! —Linda

5 1/2 cups water

2 1/2 cups brown rice

1 teaspoon low sodium salt

3 cups soy milk creamer or soy milk

1/4 cup pure maple syrup

1 teaspoon vanilla

Dash cinnamon

Fresh fruit of your choice, cut into bite size pieces

Nuts of your choice

Yield: 10 cups

(1/2 cup) Calories 132 Total Fat 3g Saturated Fat 0.1g Sodium 84.2mg Total Carbohydrates 23.2g Fiber 0.8g Protein 1.8g

Grammy's Crock-Pot Cake

3 cups all-purpose flour

1 tablespoon aluminum-
   free baking powder

3/4 teaspoon sea salt

2 tablespoons cornstarch

1 1/3 cup sugar

1/2 cup + 1/4 cup soy
   margarine

1 tablespoon vanilla

2 cups soy milk

5 to 8 pineapple rings

5 to 8 dried cherries

1/2 cup pecan halves

1/2 cup brown sugar

Measure flour, baking powder, salt, and cornstarch together and set aside. In a large mixing bowl, combine sugar, 1/2 cup margarine, and vanilla. Mix until smooth. Add small amounts of the soy milk and dry ingredients into the large bowl, stirring as you go until all are combined. Melt 1/4 cup margarine and pour into the Crock-Pot. Sprinkle brown sugar on top. Arrange pineapple rings, cherries, and pecans on top of the brown sugar to cover the bottom of the Crock-Pot in a pretty design. (Amount will vary depending on the size of your Crock-Pot.) Pour batter over the nuts and fruit. Turn on high and cook for 3 hours (If your Crock-Pot is smaller than 10" x 13", your cake will be deeper and take a little longer to cook.) Cake is done when toothpick inserted into center of cake comes out clean. Turn upside down onto large platter. Serve hot or cold.

Grammy Houghton, a very close friend of mine, was the first person to introduce me to a Crock-Pot cake. My dad was her pastor in Breckinridge, Texas, and every time I came for a visit, she would bake me one of her delicious cakes! She used eggs and milk in her recipe, so I tweaked it a bit. I was thrilled to discover my tweaking didn't ruin the taste at all! Although she is no longer with us, I'm sure she would be pleased to know that I included her cake in this cookbook! —Brenda

Yield: 1 cake

(1/20) Calories 229   Total Fat 8.9g   Saturated Fat 2.6g   Sodium 221.3mg   Total Carbohydrates 36.6g   Fiber 0.7g   Protein 0.6g

Pumpkin Bread Pudding

Generously spray the bottom and sides of a large Crock-Pot or slow cooker with a nonstick cooking spray. Put half of the bread cubes in the bottom and press down lightly with your hand. In a large bowl, combine the pumpkin, brown sugar, spices, and mix, then set aside. In a medium saucepan heat the soy milk just until hot. Pour into the pumpkin mixture and stir until well mixed. Pour half of the pumpkin over the bread in the Crock-Pot. Add the rest of the cubed bread on top and then pour the rest of the pumpkin mixture evenly over that. Spread around with a spoon making sure to cover all of the bread cubes. Cover and cook on low for 2 1/2 hours, until firm. Turn off the slow cooker and let the pudding sit covered for 15 to 20 minutes before serving. Serve with nondairy whipped topping.

This not only tastes good, but also makes your house smell wonderful while it is cooking. It is good served warm or cold. —Cinda

8 cups cubed whole wheat bread

3 1/2 cups vanilla soy milk

3 cups canned pumpkin

1 1/2 cups firmly packed dark brown sugar

2 1/2 teaspoons pure vanilla extract

2 teaspoons ground cinnamon

1/2 teaspoon ground ginger

1/4 teaspoon ground allspice

1/2 teaspoon ground nutmeg

1/4 teaspoon sea salt

Yield: 8 cups

(1/2 cup) Calories 199   Total Fat 1.7g   Saturated Fat 0.1g   Sodium 243.6mg   Total Carbohydrates 43.6g   Fiber 4.1g   Protein 5.4g

Crock-Pot Tips

PURCHASING A CROCK-POT

If you like the experience of walking in the door and smelling dinner cooking without you having slaved away in the kitchen preparing the meal, you'll love the convenience of a Crock-Pot. Take a few minutes in the morning before work or school to throw some ingredients into the pot, set it, and forget it. When you come home at dinnertime, you'll be greeted by the aroma of an easy dinner.

Crock-Pots have been around for years; today, in response to the busy lives we lead, they are more popular than ever. The newest Crock-Pots on the market come with divided liners, timers to adjust the cooking start time. The newer appliances seem to get hotter than models only a few years old, so it's best to learn how your particular Crock-Pot cooks.

HERE ARE SOME THINGS TO CONSIDER BEFORE PURCHASING A CROCK-POT

Consider the Size of Your Family

Crock-Pots range in size from 1 pint all the way up to 7-quart capacity. Small Crock-Pots will feed 1 to 2 people nicely, but for a crowd you'll need a bigger appliance. Remember that the Crock-Pot must be filled 1/2 to 2/3 full for best cooking results.

Used or New?

If purchasing a "used" Crock-Pot, check to be sure it is heating properly. You can do that by testing the temperature of food with a thermometer while it is cooking. The low setting should be about 200 degrees, and the high setting 300 degrees. Note that both of these temperatures are well above the minimum safe temperature of 140 degrees. The benefit of buying used is obviously price, however there are new ones at very reasonable prices as well.

What Features?

The features in a Crock-Pot range from simply plugging in and selecting high and low to programmable features including a delayed start, keep warm features, and temperature variations. If this is your first Crock-Pot, buy a simple version.

Shape: Oval or Round?

Aesthetics and personal preference are the considerations here. Shape is a personal choice and can be based upon the size of the space where you will be storing it, as well as what you think looks good on your counter.

Construction

Be sure that you are buying an actual Crock-Pot, which has the heating element in the sides of the appliance, not just in the bottom. And always look for a Crock-Pot that has a removable liner. This makes cleaning much easier, because the liners are usually stoneware and dishwasher safe. A Crock-Pot with a nonremovable liner should usually be lined with a cooking bag for easier cleanup.

BENEFITS OF CROCK-POT COOKING

- A Crock-Pot doesn't heat up the kitchen nearly as much as the stovetop or oven, so it's a perfect hot weather cooking appliance. It also uses less energy so you save on your electric bill!

- It frees up space in oven and stovetop and is great to use for parties, large gatherings, or doing a large cooking session for the freezer.

- Food tastes well blended because flavors have time to develop while your meal slowly cooks all day.

- It can be used on a buffet table for serving hot

foods such as soup, stew, sauces, meatballs in spaghetti sauce, etc.

GENERAL CROCK-POT TIPS

Crock-Pots are best if used for recipes with a high water content like spaghetti sauce, soup, chili and stew. However, more and more recipes foods like puddings and cakes are being created specifically for slow cookers!

For best results, fill the crock at least half full with food and/or liquid. Leave at least one to two inches of empty space at the top beneath the lid to allow for the food to bubble when it reaches a simmer. Also, the food will not cook properly if filled too full! Under-fill the slow cooker and your recipe will be overdone. Overfill the slow cooker and your food will "spit out" of the slow cooker and additional time will need to be added. Remember: Food expands when it is heated.

Resist the urge to peek! Lifting the lid adds time to the cooking process by letting heat out. Add 15 to 20 minutes to the cooking time for each time you lift the lid to peek or stir. Stirring usually isn't required during slow cooking on low heat. You might want to stir once or twice during the last hour, but remember to add cooking time. Two stirring sessions equal a minimum of half an hour longer cooking.

Vegetables such as carrots and potatoes should be added to the bottom of the Crock-Pot. Hard vegetables need a longer cooking time, and the bottom is the first part of the cooker to heat up, so they'll start cooking sooner.

Add spices near the end of the cooking time. They will lose flavor if cooked with the rest of the ingredients for the long cooking period. Use whole leaf herbs and spices instead of ground for better flavor. Some spices, especially cayenne pepper, can become bitter over a long cooking time. Add those in the last hour of cooking for best flavor.

Always include liquids in all Crock-Pot cooking recipes. Liquids do not boil away in the slow cooker, so if you are making a recipe that wasn't specifically developed for the Crock-Pot, reduce the liquid by 1/3 to 1/2 unless you are cooking rice or making soup.

Remove the cover by opening away from your face. The steam is hot enough to burn badly.

Keep the crock covered while cooking. The lid on a crock doesn't provide a tight seal (it isn't suppose to), but it's important to keep the lid in the center of the crock for best results.

Pasta and rice can be cooked in a Crock-Pot. Pasta needs lots of liquid to cook properly, and should be added during the last hour of cooking time, depending on the consistency you prefer. Converted rice can be cooked in the Crock-Pot just like vegetables or meat. Make sure you have enough liquid in the recipe so the rice becomes tender.

You can make cakes and desserts in the Crock-Pot! Use a small round rack or vegetable steamer to lift the cake pan off the bottom of the Crock-Pot so heat circulates evenly around the pan. You do need a larger Crock-Pot for baking cakes and other desserts. A 5-quart slow cooker will hold an 8" or 9" cake pan or springform pan.

You may need to increase cooking times if you live at a high altitude, usually by 40–50 percent.

COOKING FROZEN FOODS WARNING

Many people cook frozen foods in the Crock-Pot. And others like to reheat foods in the Crock-Pot. Most food experts do not recommend these practices, because foods need to reach a temperature of 140 degrees within 1 1/2 hours to prevent bacteria growth. Even if the foods do eventually reach a safe temperature and cook thoroughly, bacteria in the food can produce toxins that aren't destroyed by heat and they can make you sick. Many people have experienced food poisoning and don't even know it. They may have some digestive discomfort or feel ill for a day or two and then recover. Unfortunately, a person in a high-risk group (elderly, persons with compromised immune systems, small children, and pregnant women) can suffer serious consequences from food poisoning. More than 5,000 people die each year in the U.S. as a result of food poisoning. If you decide to cook frozen foods or reheat foods in the Crock-Pot, do so at your own risk. One thing you can do is to warm the liquid used in the recipe and add it along with the frozen foods, to help raise the temperature more quickly. Taking a calculated risk may be acceptable to you as long as you know the consequences and as long as no member of your family is in a high-risk group.

RECIPE MODIFICATIONS

Recipes intended for other cooking methods must be modified for slow cookers. Often water must be decreased, as ordinary cooking at higher temperatures requires enough liquid to allow for evaporation, while slow cookers prevent vapor loss. With some experience, timing and recipe adjustments can be successfully made for many recipes not originally intended for these cookers. If excessive liquid is present at the end of cooking, it can be reduced and concentrated by rapid boiling in a saucepan.

CONVERTING RECIPES

Many recipes can be converted to cook in the Crock-Pot. Soups and stews, of course, are natural slow cooker favorites. Casseroles benefit from the low temperatures and even cooking heat. Reduce the amount of liquid a recipe calls for, since liquids do not evaporate during Crock-Pot cooking. However, if you are cooking rice, beans, or pasta, don't reduce the liquid called for. You generally need twice as much liquid as product to cook these ingredients. Below is a chart converting oven and stovetop cooking times to Crock-Pot-cooking times.

Oven or stovetop cooking time	Crock-Pot (low) cooking time	Crock-Pot (high) cooking time
15 to 30 min.	4 to 6 hrs.	1 1/2 to 2 1/2 hrs.
35 to 45 min.	6 to 8 hrs.	3 to 4 hrs.
50 min. to 3 hrs.	8 to 16 hrs.	4 to 6 hrs.

PREPARING INGREDIENTS

Vegetables should be cut or chopped roughly the same size and placed in the bottom of the Crock-Pot for more even cooking. Dried beans, with the exception of lentils and split peas, should be soaked overnight prior to cooking in a Crock-Pot. The soaking water should be discarded and new water added.

FOR YOUR HEALTH

Studies have shown that the low, constant heat Crock-Pots cook by may help prevent disease! Some compounds called "advanced glycation end products" are formed when sugars, fats, and proteins are heated at high temperatures, as when food is grilled, broiled, or microwaved. These AGE's irritate cells and may be a factor in the formation of heart disease, cancer, and diabetes. Since slow cookers heat less than 300 degrees, fewer of these compounds form in Crock-Pot cooked meals.

TO CLEAN A CROCK-POT

Fill the appliance with hot soapy water when the cooker has cooled. Let soak for 15 to 20 minutes, and then scrub with a cloth, nylon net pad, or a plastic sponge. Do not use a harsh abrasive cleaner, SOS pad, or metal pad. Rinse well in hot water and dry.

To remove mineral stains, fill Crock-Pot 3/4 full with hot water and 1 cup white vinegar. Cover and cook on high for 2 hours. Then let the Crock-Pot cool and soak and clean as directed above.

To remove water marks from glazed crockery, rub the surface with vegetable oil and let stand for 2 to 3 hours. Then fill with hot soapy water, rub the surface, and scrub with a nylon net pad. Rinse and dry well.

DEFINITION OF A CROCK-POT OR SLOW COOKER

From Wikipedia.com, s.v. "slow cooker," http://en.wikipedia.org/wiki/slow_cooker (accessed January 13, 2010).

A slow cooker, or Crock-Pot (a trademark that is often used generically in the U.S.A.), or Slo-Cooker (a trade mark that is often used generically in the UK), is a countertop electrical cooking appliance that maintains a relatively low temperature (compared to other cooking methods like baking, boiling, and frying) for many hours, allowing unattended cooking of soups, stews and other suitable dishes.

DESIGN

A slow cooker consists of a lidded round or oval cooking pot made of glazed ceramic or porcelain, surrounded by a housing, usually metal, containing a thermostatically controlled electric heating element. The lid is often transparent glass and is seated in a groove in the pot edge; condensed vapor collects in that groove and provides a low-pressure seal to the atmosphere. Pressure inside a working Crock-Pot is therefore effectively at atmospheric pressure, despite the water vapor generated inside the pot. A Crock-Pot therefore is substantially different from a pressure cooker and presents no danger of an abrupt (perhaps explosive) pressure release.

The ceramic pot, or a "crock," acts as both a cooking container and a heat reservoir. Slow cookers come in a variety of sizes, from 500 mL (16 ounce) to 7 liters (7.4 quarts). Due to the placement of heating elements (generally at the bottom and often also partway up the sides), there is usually a minimum recommended liquid level to avoid uncontrolled local heating.

Many slow cookers have two or more temperature settings (e.g., low, medium, high, and sometimes a "keep warm" setting). A typical slow cooker is designed to heat food to 170°F (77°C) on low, to perhaps 190 to 200°F (88 to 93°C) on high. Many recipes that include sauce or liquid will reach the boiling point around the edges, while food in the center remains gently cooked. This is because slow cooker settings are based on wattage, not temperature. Some slow cookers sold in the U.S. in the past several decades did not change temperature, regardless of setting, at all; each setting brought the contents to full heat, with the only difference in setting being the duration of heating. This may have been due to concerns about product liability from unsafe food holding temperatures.

OPERATION

Raw food, and a liquid which is predominantly water or vegetable stock, but not oil without water, are placed in the slow cooker. Some recipes call for preheated liquid. The cooker lid is put on and the cooker is switched on. Cookers often have high and low heat thermostat settings. Some cookers automatically switch from cooking to warming (maintaining the temperature at 160°F to 165°F [71°C to 74°C] after a fixed time or after the internal temperature of the food, as determined by a probe, reaches a given goal.

The heating element heats the contents to a steady temperature in the 175°F to 200°F (79°C to 93°C) range. The contents are enclosed by the crock and the lid, and attain an essentially constant temperature. The vapor that is produced at this temperature condenses on the lid and returns as liquid. Some water-soluble vitamins are leaked into the liquid, but mostly remain in the broth.

The liquid transfers heat from the pot walls to its contents, and also distributes flavors. A lid must be used to prevent warm vapor from escaping, taking heat with it, typically faster than it is replaced, thus cooling the contents, perhaps dangerously.

Basic cookers, which have only high, med, low, or keep warm settings, have to be manually turned on and off. This means the cook must be present at the end of the cooking time. More advanced cookers have settings for high and low (e.g., 4 hours high, 8 hours low) which allows the cook to choose a cooking time after which the cooker switches to "keep warm" mode. The most advanced cookers have computerized timing devices that allow the cook to programmed the cooker to perform multiple operations (e.g., 2 hours high, followed by 2 hours low, followed by warm) and to delay the start of cooking.

Because they stay warm for a long time, slow cookers are a staple of potlucks and other social meals. To cater to this use, many companies now offer methods of sealing the lid on during transport (normally with elastic bands or clamps) to prevent the contents from spilling.

HAZARDS

Slow cookers are less dangerous than ovens or stove tops due to the lower temperatures and closed lids. However, they still contain several pounds/kilograms of near boiling temperature food and liquid, and like any such are capable of causing serious burns if spilled. They are not invariably safe around children and pets as a consequence. In addition, since they contain heating elements, it is possible to cause a fire if slow cookers are misused. For instance, in slow cookers with two heating elements, one heating element can be out of contact with the liquid due to insufficient liquid or food and so cause local overheating, perhaps cracking the ceramic pot or melting or deforming a metal one.

References:
Linda Larsen, "Crockpot 101," About.com: Busy Cooks, http:busycooks.about.com/od/ slowcookerrecipes/a/crockpot101.htm (accessed January 13, 2010).

Resources

BUTLER FOODS is an independent, family owned business. Their products are plant-based and no animal by products. They make Soy Curls and Chik-Style Seasoning. Visit their Web site to order online or to find out where their products are sold in your area.

Web site: **www.butlerfoods.com**
Phone: (503) 879-5005
Address: Butler Foods
P.O. Box 40, Grand Ronde, OR 97347

YVES VEGGIE CUISINE produces healthy vegetarian soy meat substitutes that are not only packed with good nutrition and flavor but are low in fat and calories. One of the things we love best is the texture, and also that it doesn't have an overwhelming flavor. It takes on whatever flavor you give it and has no aftertaste that can be common with other products.

Web site: **www.yvesveggie.com**
Phone: 1-800-434-4246

COUNTRY LIFE NATURAL FOODS offers a line of natural, whole and organic foods at reasonable prices. They carry most of the specialty items in this cookbook such as Mori-Nu Tofu, Mori-Nu Mates, McKay's Chicken and Beef Seasonings, Bragg Liquid Aminos, Vegex, Emes Kosher gelatin, pure maple syrup, whole grains, herbs, spices, and more than 1,200 other natural items. They will ship directly to your house via UPS. Ask for their free catalog.

Web site: **www.clnf.org**
Phone: 1-800-456-7694

FOLLOW YOUR HEART is located at Canoga Park, California. They offer Grapeseed Oil Vegenaise and the original Vegenaise. In our opinion this is one of the best nondairy mayonnaises on the market.

Web site: **www.followyourheart.com**
Phone: (818) 725-2820

BETTER THAN MILK soy milk is one of our favorites. We have used it in a lot of our recipes.

E-mail: info@betterthanmilk.com
Phone: 1-800-227-2320

CREATIVE FOODS INC.

Web site: **www.creativefoodsinc.com**
E-mail: sales@creativefoodsinc.com
buenocoffee@yahoo.com
Message: (541) 504-1463
Cell: (541) 788-3663 (Yollie)
Address: Creative Foods Inc.
460 NE Hemlock Ave, Suite B, Redmond, OR 97756

TOFUTTI offers a variety of nondairy items that are soy based and Casein free. They offer Sour Supreme, Cream Cheese, Cheddar Cheese, Mozzarella Cheese, Cheese Slices and much more.

Web site: **www.tofutti.com**
E-mail: info@tofutti.com
Phone: (908) 272-2400
Address: Tofutti Brands, Inc.
50 Jackson Dr., Cranford, NJ 07016

THE VEGETARIAN EXPRESS offers a wide variety of seasonings as well as prepackaged products such as cookie mixes, pasta mixes, gravies, waffles, etc. We've tried many of them and they are excellent! Their oatmeal cookie mix is incredible, and we use many of their seasonings in our recipes.

Web site: **www.thevegetarianexpress.com**
Phone: (734) 355-3593
Address: P.O. Box 33, South Lyon, MI 48178

MCKAY'S SEASONING We use their chicken and beef seasonings in many of our recipes. Our Mom cooked with them when we were little girls and we still love their seasoning today. Their beef seasoning has recently changed and we like it even better than before. We think you will too!

Web site: **www.mckays-seasoning.com**
Phone: (419) 531-8963
Address: 336 N. Westwood Ave., Toledo, OH 43607

WESTSOY has a good line of different seasoned Seitan—wheat protein. We use the traditionally seasoned wheat protein.

Phone: 1-800-434-4246, Monday through Friday, 7 a.m. to 5 p.m. Mountain Time
Address: WestSoy Consumer Relations
The Hain Celestial Group
4600 Sleepytime Dr., Boulder, CO 80301

DELIGHT FOODS makes our favorite vegan chicken, called Delight Soy Nuggets. They also make a beef and turkey substitute.

Web site: **www.delightsoy.com**
E-mail: info@delightsoy.com
Phone: (919) 468-1077
Address: 1317 Copeland Oak Dr., Morrisville, NC 27511

THREE ANGELS BROADCASTING NETWORK (3ABN) For more information on healthy living, check the 3ABN Web site. You can view vegan cooking programs and receive additional recipes on 3ABN Television or 3ABN Radio online 24 hours a day. They offer a number of programs on health and its benefits.

Web site: **www.3abn.org**
E-mail: mail@3abn.org
Phone: 618-627-4651
Address: P.O. Box 220, West Frankfort, IL 62896

NEWSTART LIFESTYLE CENTER will give you more information about healthy living.

Web site: **www.newstart.com**
Phone: 1-800-525-9192
Address: Weimar Institute Newstart Life Center
P.O. Box 486, Weimar, CA 95736

Substitutions

MILK SUBSTITUTES

Soy Good is a vegan soymilk by Dressler's, and one of our favorites. There are two kinds: plain and simple, which is good for soups and gravies, and the regular vanilla Soy Good, which has a green label and is good for anything that requires a sweeter taste. For more information, check our resource page.

Better Than Milk original flavor is great to cook with and is great for cold cereals. The vanilla flavor is good for cookies, cakes, and baked goods.

Nondairy whipped topping is a milk-free item that can be found in most of your local grocery stores. If the grocery store does not offer this product, be sure and ask them to carry it.

NATURAL SWEETENERS

Florida Crystals is milled sugarcane and can be used as white sugar one cup for one cup. It is our choice for many recipes, but especially those that need to be light in color.

Pure maple syrup is inexpensive if purchased at large membership stores. Use in muffins, breads, cookies, pancakes, fruit smoothies, and desserts.

Frozen fruit juices are all-natural sweeteners. Just be sure the label says 100 percent juice. Use in fruit sauces, pies, smoothies, and baked goods.

Sucanat by Wholesome Foods is organic evaporated sugarcane juice with blackstrap molasses added to it. It replaces brown and white sugar one for one.

TOFU

Tofu is an excellent source of protein and contains no cholesterol. It also is an inexpensive substitute for meat, fish, poultry, and cheese.

Silken Tofu is a soybean product with a silky smooth texture. It's great for cheesecakes, pies, puddings, and salad dressings.

Water-packed tofu comes in soft, firm, or extra-firm. It has to be refrigerated and has a shorter expiration date. Water-packed tofu has a firmer, spongier texture, and it is great for things like mock scrambled eggs. It can be crumbled and will hold its shape so it is very useful in all kinds of recipes. It can be blended until smooth or sliced or baked or boiled—the ideas are endless. It is a wonderful product.

Mori-Nu Tofu does not have to be refrigerated until opened and has a long shelf life. Mori-Nu is great for making entrees, desserts, salads, salad dressings, dips, soups, mock egg salad, and many other dishes.

Mori-Nu Mates, in lemon and vanilla flavors, can be found in the health food section of large grocery stores. This product can also be purchased through Country Life Natural Foods.

OTHER PRODUCTS

Tofutti Sour Supreme is our favorite sour cream substitute. It looks and tastes close to dairy sour cream but is milk and butterfat free. It contains no cholesterol. This product can be found nationally in most health food stores and select supermarkets. Substitute this product in any recipe that calls for sour cream.

Tofutti Better Than Cream Cheese is a great substitute for cream cheese. It is milk and butterfat free and contains no cholesterol. It is great for making entrées, desserts, or just used as a spread for bagels.

Grapeseed Oil Vegenaise and Original Vegenaise, both by Follow Your Heart, are great mayonnaise replacements. Grapeseed oil is an excellent natural source of vitamin E and essential fatty acids necessary for normal cell metabolism and maintenance. Vegenaise is found only in the refrigerated sections of your grocery stores.

Bragg Liquid Aminos is an unfermented soy sauce replacement. It can be used in entrées, Oriental foods, to marinate gravies, and in any recipe that calls for soy sauce.

Brewer's yeast flakes are made of nutritional yeast, which is one of the most perfect foods known. It is a powerful health source of B vitamins, amino acids, proteins, minerals, enzymes, and nucleic acids. This premium yeast is grown on sugar beets, which are known to absorb nutrients from the soil faster than almost any other crop. As a result, this yeast is exceptionally rich in selenium, chromium, potassium, copper, manganese, iron, zinc, and other factors natural to yeast. It is also gluten free. This yeast can be used as a breading, in entrées, or sprinkled on top of foods like popcorn, tofu scrambled eggs, and so forth.

Carob chips are a great alternative to chocolate chips. Some carob chips have dairy and lots of sweeteners in them, so look for the vegan ones sweetened with barley malt. These can be found in your local co-ops, health food stores, or larger grocery stores.

Rumford's Baking Powder is an aluminum-free baking powder.

Egg substitute: 1 tablespoon of cornstarch can be used as an egg replacer.

Soy margarine may be found in your local grocery store. Find a brand that is vegan, non-hydrogenated and has no trans fats and no cholesterol.

Pecan meal is simply pecans that have been ground into a fine meal. This product can usually be found in your local grocery store or purchased at larger grocery stores. To make your own, just put the pecans in the blender and blend until it is the right consistency. Walnuts can be substituted in any of our recipes that call for pecans.

Vege-Sal is a seasoned salt that is available in the health food section of most grocery stores.

Time-saving Tips

KEEP A WELL-STOCKED PANTRY

To successfully put together meals in minutes, you need a well-stocked pantry, refrigerator, and freezer. In other words, keep on hand ingredients that are used often and can be combined easily for simple and delicious meals. Then all you need to do is shop for fresh ingredients as needed. Many who are just learning the joys of cooking often ask us what foods we stock in our pantries, refrigerators, and freezers. Below are some of our suggestions.

Basic Pantry Items:

Whole wheat flour—white, regular, pastry

Sugar, brown sugar

Pure maple syrup

Aluminum-free baking powder

Baking soda

Oats

Rice

Dried pastas

Canned and dried fruits, vegetables, beans

Peanut butter

Dried beans and lentils

Canned tomato sauces

Canned soups

Carob chips

Honey

Vegetable oil, olive oil

Nonstick cooking spray

Dried gluten products

Other food items that have a long shelf life

Of course, any serious cook will always have fresh potatoes stored in a cool, dark place.

Basic Seasonings:

Salt

Vegetarian chicken and beef seasonings

Dried parsley, basil, thyme, oregano, rosemary, dill, sage

Chili powder

Garlic powder

Onion powder

Cayenne pepper

Cumin

Minced onion

Ground cinnamon, ginger, cloves, nutmeg

Basic Refrigerator Items:

Soy margarine

Soymilk

Ketchup

Mustard

Grapeseed Oil Vegenaise

Water-packed tofu

Bottled lemon juice

Bragg Liquid Aminos

Vegan Worcestershire sauce

Apples, oranges, and—yes—onions!

Basic Freezer Items:

Pecans, almonds, walnuts

Apple and orange juice concentrates

Vegetables and fruits

Vegetarian meat substitutes

GROCERY LISTS

Place an ongoing grocery list in a convenient place in your kitchen and add items as they need to be replenished. (Be sure and take it with you while grocery shopping.)

FRUITS AND VEGETABLES

Only purchase fresh fruits and vegetables that will be used within 2 to 3 days. (Kept longer than that they lose not only freshness and taste but nutritional benefits as well.)

Fruit Facts: Bananas, apricots, cantaloupe, kiwi, nectarines, peaches, pears, plantains, and plums continue to ripen after they're picked. Fruits that you should pick or buy ripe and ready-to-eat include apples, cherries, grapefruit, grapes, oranges, pineapples, strawberries, tangerines, and watermelon. To speed up the ripening of fruits such as peaches, pears, and plums, put them in a ripening bowl or in a loosely closed brown paper bag at room temperature. Plastic bags don't work for ripening.

Bananas: Keep bananas fresh a little longer by storing them in the refrigerator after they've reached the desired degree of ripeness. The outside will turn brown, but they will be delicious!

Onions: Place chopped onions in small freezer bags and store in the freezer so they are ready to use in an instant! They work best in recipes that require cooking or baking and in most cases do not need to be thawed before using! A tip to decrease the tears when peeling onions—store onions in the refrigerator!

Garlic: To mince garlic without having it stick to your knife, add a few drops of water to the garlic and then chop. The garlic sticks to the cutting board and not your knife.

Lemons: To get the most juice, roll them on the counter with the palm of your hand. This will help free the juice. If you have too many lemons and don't want them to go bad, slice them into quarters and freeze in an airtight freezer bag or freezer-safe container. You can take out a little or a lot of lemon, depending upon your needs.

Fresh Herbs: Use kitchen scissors for mincing fresh herbs. It's faster than a knife. Wash and dry fresh herbs with a salad spinner.

Fresh Ginger: To peel fresh ginger quickly, scrape with the edge of the bowl of a spoon. This will remove the peel, leaving most of the ginger for use.

COOKING TIPS

When cooking vegetables, start with the veggies that take the longest to cook and keep adding, ending up with the ones that cook the fastest. A general rule of thumb would be to start with aromatics such as onions, celery, and carrots, followed by denser options such as broccoli or cauliflower, peppers, then less dense veggies such as zucchini and mushrooms, and ending with greens such as spinach and chard.

FOOD PREP

Shorten food prep time by buying already prepped vegetables such as shredded carrots, sliced mushrooms, fresh chopped onions, shredded lettuce, washed green beans, or bagged broccoli florets, etc.

TIME-SAVING GADGETS

(In no particular order of importance): Kitchen scissors, garlic press, pastry blender, sharp knifes, miniature food processor, four-sided grater, handheld blender, cookie cutter, lemon zester, citrus juicer, heat-resistant rubber spatulas, tongs, wire whisks, measuring cups and spoons, good quality vegetable peeler, digital timer, salad spinner, colander, flexible plastic cutting board, and rolling pin. Don't forget a variety of sized stainless steel scoops—the kind where you push a lever on the handle.

LARGER TIME-SAVING KITCHEN TOOLS

Rice cooker, electric Crock-Pot, electric food processor, electric knife, and pressure cooker.

PLAN MEALS AHEAD OF TIME

Make out weekly menus and save time and money! Also make cooking time family bonding time! Include the kids when preparing food and you'll not only be making delicious recipes, but you'll be making lifelong memories! And picky eaters will usually taste what they have helped prepare.

- Nonperishable foods such as cakes and cookies can be prepared a few days in advance and will still taste good. Or they can be frozen for longer storage.

- Limit the number of foods served for each meal. Prepare most perishable foods no more than 1 day prior to a meal. One-dish meals can usually be prepared a day in advance, refrigerated, and then baked just prior to your dinner. Add 15 to 20 additional minutes for heating.

- Cut washed fruits and vegetables for salads, relish trays, and stir-fry recipes ahead of time, but only 24 hours ahead at most. Celery and carrot sticks stay crisp when covered with crushed ice and refrigerated.

- Always wash fruits and vegetables with cool running water and then cover in one-time use plastic bags or storage containers. Refrigerate as soon as possible after washing and cutting. Keep apples, pears, bananas, and peaches from turning brown by coating them with a citrus juice such as lemon, orange, or pineapple. Bananas will turn brown faster than other fruits.

- Assemble all of your ingredients before starting a recipe. Be sure to read your recipe over carefully. This will save you the frustration of starting to prepare your recipe only to discover that you are missing some important ingredients!

- Don't be in too much of a hurry. Taste will be enhanced if you allow time for foods to fully blend flavors. This can be achieved by preparing food at least 30 minutes prior to serving. (This includes not only foods served hot but cold foods as well, such as pasta and fruit salads, potato salad, salad dressings, cold soups, etc.)

LAST BUT NOT LEAST

If you are trying a new recipe for the first time, follow it exactly! This way you will know how it is suppose to taste. Make any changes the second time.

Measurements & Equivalents

3 teaspoons	=	1 tablespoon
4 tablespoons	=	1/4 cup
5 tablespoons + 1 teaspoon	=	1/3 cup
8 tablespoons	=	1/2 cup
12 tablespoons	=	3/4 cup
16 tablespoons	=	1 cup
1 tablespoon	=	1/2 fluid ounce
1 cup	=	8 fluid ounces
2 cups	=	1 pint
4 cups / 2 pints	=	1 quart
4 quarts	=	1 gallon

1 teaspoon	=	5 milliliters (mL)
1 tablespoon	=	15 milliliters
1 fluid ounce	=	30 milliliters
2 fluid ounces	=	60 milliliters
8 fluid ounces (1 cup)	=	240 milliliters
16 fluid ounces (1 pint)	=	480 milliliters
32 fluid ounces (1 quart)	=	960 milliliters
128 fluid ounces (1 gallon)	=	3.785 liters

WEIGHT
Metric equivalents rounded

1/4 ounce	7 grams
1/2 ounce	14 grams
1 ounce	28 grams
4 ounces	113 grams
8 ounces (1/2 pound)	227 grams
16 ounces (1 pound)	454 grams
32 ounces (2 pounds)	907 grams
40 ounces (2 1/4 pounds)	1.13 kilograms

OVEN TEMPERATURE
Celsius equivalents rounded

Fahrenheit	Celsius	Gas setting
275 degrees	135 degrees	Mark 1
300 degrees	150 degrees	Mark 2
325 degrees	165 degrees	Mark 3
350 degrees	180 degrees	Mark 4
375 degrees	190 degrees	Mark 5
400 degrees	205 degrees	Mark 6
425 degrees	220 degrees	Mark 7
450 degrees	235 degrees	Mark 8
475 degrees	245 degrees	Mark 9
Broil		Grill

Index

Index (CONTINUED)